2030 AGENDA

DEPOPULATION,

America's Last Stand

Awakening the Unbound from the Conspiracy of Control

Author J. Brevik

Printed in the United States of America

ISBN: 979-8-3485-6475-9

10 9 8 7 6 5 4 3 2 1

EMPIRE PUBLISHING
www.empirebookpublishing.com

Contents

The Illusion of Freedom

The roar of the crowd echoed through the packed stadium as tens of thousands of people cheered, their voices rising in unison. The championship game was in full swing, and for the citizens gathered in the stands, it was the highlight of the year. Every eye was glued to the field, every breath held in anticipation of the next play. Above them, a dazzling display of fireworks lit up the night sky, each explosion drawing gasps of awe from the spectators.

But not everyone was captivated by the spectacle.

Jackson Rivers, seated near the stadium's edge, barely noticed the game. His attention drifted from the cheering fans to the massive digital screens projecting the event across the city. It wasn't just sports that gripped the nation's attention—concerts, television shows, and flashy entertainment events consumed the lives of nearly everyone around him. The government had perfected the art of distraction.

It was all a carefully crafted illusion.

"Keep them entertained and keep them blind," Jackson muttered, a slight smile tugging at his lips as he took in the scene around him. Every cheer, every chant, was a reminder of how easily the public could be pacified. The so- called "Land of the Free" had become a masterfully orchestrated prison where the masses were fed a steady diet of entertainment to keep them docile, distracted, and obedient.

Jackson wasn't like the others, though. He had seen behind the curtain and discovered what lay beneath the shiny exterior of this false reality. He glanced up at the flashing billboards advertising the latest TV shows and streaming services. Slogans like "Escape Reality" and "Live for the Moment" scrolled across the screens in bold, enticing fonts. To most, it was harmless fun. To Jackson, it was a reminder of just how deep the government's claws had sunk into the minds of the people.

A vibration in his pocket pulled him from his thoughts. Pulling out his phone, he opened a secure messaging app. A single notification blinked—a new message from a contact he only knew as "Specter." He tapped it open, glancing around to ensure no one was watching.

"Tonight. The truth awaits. Be ready."

Jackson's pulse quickened as he slipped the phone back into his pocket. He had been following Specter's trail for months now, unraveling pieces of a dark puzzle that exposed a system designed not to serve the people but to control them. Each new revelation was worse than the last, casting doubt on everything he thought he knew.

The crowd's sudden roar jolted him back to the present. A player had scored, and the stadium erupted in a frenzy of applause. Jackson stood up, blending in with the cheering fans, clapping along with a faint smile. But behind his eyes, there was a fire that wouldn't be quenched—a determination to expose the truth and tear down the false reality.

As he made his way toward the exit, Jackson knew tonight would mark the beginning of something new. People might be entranced by their screens and distractions, but they weren't beyond reach. It was time to shatter the illusion and show them what true freedom meant.

For now, the government could keep its games and flashing lights.

But soon, the curtain would fall

The Pandemic of Deception

In the year 2020, the world stood paralyzed by an unseen enemy. A mysterious virus, COVID-19, swept across the globe, leaving fear and uncertainty in its wake. Or so the story went. The government, aided by a complicit media machine, had woven an elaborate narrative—a tapestry of fear designed not to protect the people, but to control them. Behind closed doors, the truth was far more sinister. The so-called pandemic was little more than a convenient rebranding of the common influenza, its name carefully selected to evoke dread and urgency. COVID-19 wasn't a natural disaster. It was a calculated operation. Scientists and technocrats had spent years working in secret, preparing for this moment. The virus was merely the smokescreen for the real objective: introducing RNA- altering technology into the human population.

The government's agenda was clear to those who dared to look beyond the surface. The RNA-based injections were heralded as humanity's salvation, a miraculous solution to a manufactured crisis. But they were, in truth, the first phase of a global transformation—a program designed to integrate every human being into a digital network, where their thoughts, emotions, and behaviors could be monitored and manipulated. This wasn't about saving lives; it was about gaining control.

Fear was the weapon of choice. Governments rolled out relentless campaigns of hysteria. Death counts flashed on every screen. Lockdowns turned cities into ghost towns. Social interaction became a crime, and questioning the narrative became tantamount to treason. The people were bombarded with messages of compliance: "Trust the science. Take the shot. Save lives." Fear silenced dissent and blinded the masses to the encroaching chains.

Even now, years later, the scars of that campaign linger. Facemasks, once a symbol of collective fear, still cover the faces of many. They've become a permanent fixture for those who believe in the false sickness without question, clinging to the lies they've been told. Despite overwhelming evidence that the narrative was fabricated, millions remain captive to the illusion. For them, the facemask is not just fabric—it is a shield, a symbol of trust in the authorities that deceived them.

The campaign to suppress dissent was ruthless. Even doctors, risking everything to speak out, were silenced. Many ordered vials of COVID-19 for independent analysis, hoping to uncover the truth. But they were blocked at every turn. Their findings were censored, their data erased, and their voices drowned in a sea of propaganda. Social media platforms became weapons in the war on truth. YouTube, Facebook, and other tech giants, guided by artificial intelligence designed to detect and delete dissent, erased videos, posts, and accounts exposing the lies.

For those lucky enough to stumble across the truth, it was often fleeting—a post that disappeared minutes after being shared, a video taken down before it could gain traction. Only the first few viewers managed to see the evidence before it vanished into digital oblivion. Websites engineered with advanced AI algorithms hunted down and destroyed anything that challenged the official narrative.

Countless lawsuits were filed by courageous doctors, desperately trying to inform the public about the deception.

They faced insurmountable odds: courts that dismissed their cases, media outlets that branded them as conspiracy theorists, and a society too conditioned by fear to question the status quo. These whistleblowers weren't fighting for fame or fortune—they were fighting for the people, for the right to know the truth.

But the truth was not an easy pill to swallow. For decades, the government had laid the groundwork for this moment by flooding daily life with chemicals designed to dull the mind and weaken the spirit. From the food people consumed to the air they breathed and the water they drank, toxins infiltrated every aspect of life. These chemicals didn't just degrade the body—they robbed people of the mental capacity to make educated decisions.

The result was a population so intellectually stunted, so utterly oblivious to reality, that they became incapable of questioning authority. They were, in essence, dumb as dog shit. And worse yet, they would fight to the death to defend their ignorance. Even when presented with undeniable evidence of their error, they clung to their delusions with an almost religious fervor. For these people, being right wasn't about truth—it was about ego. Ask any of them, and they'd tell you: they were always right. Idiots always are.

Yet, the injections didn't merely alter the body—they altered the very essence of humanity. The RNA particles introduced subtle changes, targeting the nervous system and the brain. Dreams became strangely vivid, yet disjointed. People experienced heightened anxiety, impulsive anger, or even an eerie emotional numbness. Few connected these changes to the injections. Most attributed them to the stress of the pandemic.

But the changes were deliberate. Each dose brought humanity closer to a critical threshold—the moment when NeuroLink would be fully activated. The architects of this program called it "The Great Reset," a term designed to sound hopeful. In truth, it was a reset of free will itself. Humanity would no longer be independent but instead would function as nodes in a vast network, controlled by algorithms and monitored by unseen powers.

Distraction was the key to success. Entertainment, political theater, and social media fueled division and kept the population docile. Concerts, streaming platforms, and sporting events resumed, becoming opiates for a society on the brink of transformation. The people didn't realize they were being pacified while the last remnants of their autonomy were stripped away.

Yet, not everyone succumbed. A small but growing resistance began to form—doctors, scientists, and ordinary citizens who pieced together the fragments of truth. They were labeled conspiracy theorists, their voices drowned out by a flood of propaganda. Algorithms silenced their warnings, and society mocked their courage. But they persisted.

The resistance discovered that the injections weren't the end—they were the beginning. The chemicals flooding their bodies weren't just altering RNA; they were targeting the pineal gland, humanity's ancient connection to intuition and higher consciousness. Fluoride in the water, toxins in the food, and now RNA in the blood—all were part of a coordinated effort to sever humanity from its spiritual essence.

Those who resisted understood the stakes. If NeuroLink went fully online, the human race would become slaves to a digital overlord, unable to think or act freely. It wasn't just a battle for survival—it was a battle for the soul of humanity.

The government, however, had underestimated one crucial force: the indomitable human spirit. Whispers of rebellion began to echo in the darkness, a quiet defiance against the rising tide of control. From hidden basements to encrypted online forums, the seeds of revolution were sown.

The question now was simple: Could humanity awaken in time? Or would the chains of technology bind them forever?

A Glimpse Behind the Curtain

Jackson slipped out of the stadium, blending seamlessly into the stream of fans flooding the city streets. Neon lights bathed everything in a harsh, artificial glow, making it almost impossible to tell night from day. The towering screens on every corner blared with highlights from the game while celebrities grinned and sang from billboards, urging the public to indulge in everything from fast food to fashion trends.

He kept his head down and his pace steady. Specter's message was vague, but the timing wasn't lost on him. Tonight was the final game of the season, a day when the entire city was tuned in, glued to their screens, or crammed into arenas like the one he had just left. It was the perfect night for something—or someone—to slip through the cracks unnoticed.

"Stay focused," Jackson murmured to himself, shoving his hands deep into his jacket pockets. He took a left turn, ducking into an alleyway that was far removed from the glittering lights of downtown. The distant hum of the crowd fell away, replaced by the muted sound of his boots against the wet pavement. He glanced up, spotting a figure leaning against the brick wall, half-shrouded in shadow.

"Specter?" he called softly.

The figure straightened and stepped forward. A hood obscured most of their face, but the faint glow from a phone screen illuminated the sharp angles of their jaw and the gleam of intense eyes. They nodded once, a gesture that was both acknowledgment and invitation.

"You're early," Specter said, voice low and gravelly. "Good. Means you're taking this seriously." Jackson stepped closer, lowering his voice. "What's the intel? You said tonight was important."Specter glanced around, then handed Jackson a small, unassuming envelope. "This. It's a glimpse of what they've been hiding. But it's only the tip of the iceberg."

Jackson took the envelope cautiously. It felt heavy, weighted with something far more important than paper. "What am I looking at here?"

"Proof," Specter replied. "Ever wonder why they push so hard to keep people watching, listening, distracted? It's not just about pacifying the masses. It's about control. You'll see it when you read it. But I'm warning you—once you see this, there's no going back."

Jackson's fingers tightened around the envelope. He'd already committed himself to this path long ago, but Specter's words still sent a chill down his spine. He knew better than most what the government was capable of, the depths of their deception. Yet, something in Specter's tone suggested this was bigger than anything he'd uncovered so far.

"What do I do once I read it?" Jackson asked, locking eyes with Specter.

The hooded figure hesitated, then took a step back. "That's up to you. But if you want to expose the truth, you're going to need allies. There's a group—small but growing. People like you, who aren't fooled by the distractions. Find them, and maybe... just maybe, we can turn this thing around."

Before Jackson could respond, Specter turned on their heel and disappeared into the shadows of the alley. The sound of their footsteps faded into silence, leaving Jackson alone.

He glanced down at the envelope in his hand. The city's distant lights and sounds felt like they belonged to a different world now. He knew he should wait until he was somewhere safer to open it, but curiosity and urgency burned inside him. With a quick glance around, he tore the envelope open.

Inside was a small flash drive and a single sheet of paper. Written in neat, precise handwriting were just a few lines of text:

Project: Elysium Protocol. Objective: Behavioral Modification through Neurochemical and Electromagnetic Stimuli.

Test Subjects: General Population.

Jackson's blood ran cold as the implications hit him. Neurochemical and electromagnetic stimuli? The crowd's rapt attention at the game, the heightened emotional responses, the near-addiction to entertainment... Could it be that all of it was engineered?

He quickly pocketed the paper and flash drive, his mind racing. Everything he'd suspected was true—and worse. The government wasn't just distracting people. They were altering them. Conditioning them to respond in predictable ways, to be more easily manipulated. Just as he was about to leave, his phone buzzed again. It was another message from Specter.

It's not just entertainment. Look at the taxation records."

Jackson frowned, then tapped his phone's screen. Specter had sent over a file labeled Comprehensive Citizen Taxation. He hesitated, then opened it. Lines of text scrolled past his screen, breaking down various categories: Federal Tax, State Tax, Property Tax, Sales Tax, Excise Tax, Gas Tax, Utility Tax, Communication Tax, and Environmental Fees. Each line contained subcategories, each more obscure and complex than the last.

"Are you kidding me?" Jackson breathed, his pulse racing as he read on. Every single transaction—from a cup of coffee to a gallon of gas—had a tax attached to it. No dollar moved without a percentage being siphoned off. He swiped to the next section: Tax on Employment Wages. It wasn't just about income tax; there were hidden deductions, social contributions, and fees that left the average citizen with a fraction of what they actually earned.

He scrolled faster, his anger building with each revelation. Even the so-called "luxury taxes" on electronics, clothing, and entertainment subscriptions funneled back into government coffers. It was a web of financial servitude, where citizens were bled dry at every turn. No matter how much they earned or how hard they worked, the system was designed to keep them indebted and enslaved.

"Everything is taxed," Jackson whispered, disbelief warring with outrage. "Even dying costs you." Funeral taxes. Burial fees. Estate taxes. Every angle was covered, ensuring that the people paid for their chains until the day they died—and beyond.

A realization struck him like a punch to the gut. They're making us pay to keep ourselves enslaved.

The glitz and glamour of the entertainment world, the constant push to consume and indulge, was nothing but a smokescreen. Every purchase, every transaction, strengthened the chains that held them down. Even those who tried to live modestly, who shunned excess, couldn't escape. The very basics—food, water, shelter—were all taxed, all controlled. They'd made it impossible to live without feeding the system that oppressed them.

Jackson's grip tightened around his phone. It wasn't just about money. It was about power. By forcing people to give up a piece of everything they owned, the government ensured that no one could ever truly be free. It wasn't just distraction or manipulation—it was slavery, hidden in plain sight.

His phone buzzed one last time. Specter's final message was short, but it carried the weight of everything Jackson had just learned.

"Find the others. And fight." Jackson took a deep breath, eyes blazing with resolve. He would find the others. And together, they would fight—because freedom wasn't something they could afford to lose. Not anymore. With one last glance at the city glowing under the weight of its own chains, Jackson turned and disappeared into the night.

Awakening the Invisible Chains

Jackson sat in the dim glow of his desk lamp, stacks of papers and books piled high around him. The room was silent except for the occasional rustle of paper and the hum of his thoughts. He had been here for hours, poring over records and piecing together fragments of a puzzle that most people never realized existed. Each page, each line of text, seemed to pull back another layer of the illusion he'd been trapped in since birth.

It all started with a question: Who am I? The answer was far more complicated than Jackson ever imagined.

His own birth certificate had been the first clue. Just a slip of paper his parents had signed without hesitation, thinking it was a simple formality. But Jackson had discovered its true purpose: it was the foundation of an invisible cage. With that signature, he had been transformed from a living being into a corporate entity, a legal fiction bound to a system designed to exploit him at every turn.

Jackson's frustration boiled over as he scribbled notes on the margins of a book, circling the same words over and over: ownership, control, fiction. Every piece of research pointed to the same truth. His name, written in all capital letters on government documents, wasn't his name at all. It was a business — a tool the system used to tie him to a web of laws and regulations that siphoned his freedom away.

"How could they hide this from us for so long?" he muttered, leaning back in his chair.

His thoughts drifted to the government's grip on every aspect of life: Social Security numbers treated as business accounts, taxes that drained wealth from every angle, even ownership of property that wasn't truly ownership at all. The deeper he dug, the more he saw how the system had transformed people into unwitting slaves, bound by invisible chains of bureaucracy and deception.

And it didn't stop there. Jackson's research had uncovered even darker truths — poisons in the food, water, and air. Chemicals designed to suppress free will and alter the very fabric of human thought. Corporations and governments working hand in hand to keep the population docile and compliant.

His heart pounded as he glanced at a map pinned to the wall, marked with red circles and lines connecting dots across the country. It was a map of forever chemicals, substances spreading silently across the land through planes, crops, and water supplies. Every trail, every arrow pointed to a deliberate strategy of control.

He remembered the headlines: cancer rates skyrocketing in rural communities, water sources tainted with chemicals too dangerous to name, and rising illnesses that doctors dismissed as coincidental. But Jackson knew better. The patterns were unmistakable. The government wasn't just failing to protect its citizens; it was deliberately poisoning them.

"Entertainment, sports, meaningless politics," he muttered, standing and pacing the room. "All distractions while they dismantle everything real."

He thought of his friends — good people, hardworking people — who spent their lives in front of glowing screens, cheering for their favorite teams or binge-watching shows designed to lull them into complacency. Meanwhile, their freedom was siphoned away, one law, one chemical, one lie at a time.

Jackson pushed back from the desk, his mind reeling. He thought of his forefathers who had fought and died for the freedoms enshrined in the Constitution. What would they think of the country now? A nation sold off piece by piece, its people turned into consumers, taxpayers, and laborers, their rights traded for illusions of comfort and safety.

But it wasn't too late. Jackson was certain of one thing: the truth was a weapon, and he intended to wield it.

First Steps to Rebellion

The morning air was crisp as Jackson stepped outside; a leather satchel slung over his shoulder. Inside were copies of the documents he had uncovered – damning evidence of government corruption, corporate collusion, and toxic control.

He had spent the night compiling everything he could: court rulings exposing secret trusts, studies on fluoride's effects on the pineal gland, and records of chemical dumps that had poisoned entire communities. His satchel was a manifesto, the first piece in a larger fight.

But Jackson knew he couldn't do this alone. He needed allies – people who saw the world the way he did, who understood the depth of the deception and were ready to act. He thought of Sarah, his childhood friend and an investigative journalist who had always had a knack for uncovering the truth. If anyone could help him expose the system, it was her.

The walk to the café where Sarah worked as a freelancer felt longer than usual. Every step carried the weight of his mission, the enormity of what he was about to set in motion.

When he arrived, she was already waiting for him, her laptop open and her coffee untouched. Her eyes lit up when she saw him, but the expression faded when she noticed his grim demeanor.

"What's going on, Jackson?" she asked, her voice low and concerned.

Jackson placed the satchel on the table and began pulling out papers. "I need your help," he said, sliding a stack of documents toward her. "This isn't just corruption. It's control, Sarah. They've turned us into slaves, and no one even realizes it."

She frowned as she skimmed the pages, her fingers tracing the lines of text. "This is… this is insane. If even half of this is true—"

"It's all true," Jackson interrupted. "And it's worse than that. They're poisoning us, keeping us distracted with entertainment while they strip away everything that matters. I need to get this out there, and you're the only person I trust."

Sarah sat back, her mind clearly racing. After a moment, she nodded. "Alright," she said. "Let's do this."

The Court of Deception

The Court System as a Corporate Entity

The judicial system, as it operates today, is not designed to dispense justice—it is designed to maintain the status quo of a corporate-run society. The courts do not uphold the Constitution; they uphold the system's profit-driven agenda. Judges, lawyers, and law enforcement are all part of a network working under corporate law, not common law. What is presented as "justice" is simply a mechanism to enforce corporate policy and extract wealth from the population.

One of the most insidious aspects of the system is its transformation of citizens into assets. As discussed, the corporate entity of the "United States" uses legal fictions—such as the "strawman" created when a birth certificate is signed—to tie every individual into its legal framework. This results in people being treated as property, or "chattel," within the corporate structure. The name on the birth certificate is not the individual's true identity, but a legal entity created for the purpose of manipulating the individual's financial and legal obligations.

Sovereign Rights vs. Corporate Authority

The sovereign rights of individuals are drowned out by the weight of corporate control. Courts, rather than serving as a place of justice, are designed to enforce corporate agendas. They follow statutory law, not common law, which has been manipulated to benefit the corporate state. In other words, the courts are nothing more than a place where the corporation's rules are enforced against the people.

As a result, individuals seeking justice find themselves lost in a web of corporate policy, facing a system that works not to solve problems but to maximize profits. This is particularly true when it comes to fines, fees, and penalties, which are often levied under false pretenses and with no real basis in law. For instance, many traffic fines and criminal charges are based on codes and statutes that have no real legal standing but are instead designed to generate revenue for the state and corporations.

The Power of Bond Claims

One of the most powerful tools in the fight against this corporate judicial system is the ability to attack the bonds of court officials. These bonds are not just a formality—they are the financial backers of the official's actions. When a judge, lawyer, or other court official violates their duty, they can be held personally liable through their bond.

For instance, if a judge acts in bad faith, ignores constitutional rights, or upholds a fraudulent ruling, individuals have the right to file a bond claim against them. This is not a simple complaint—it's a formal financial action. The bond is meant to protect the official, but when an individual proves wrongdoing, the insurance company behind the bond may be forced to pay for damages, and the bondholder may revoke the official's bond, thereby disqualifying them from holding office. This is a crucial point: when bonds are attacked, the system suffers. Judges and court officers who lose their bonds can no longer perform their duties, bringing the corporate machine to a halt, at least momentarily.

This process may seem daunting, but it is an essential method of resistance that exposes the fragility of the system.

It strips away the false sense of authority that court officials wield and serves as a reminder that they are, in fact, servants of the people, not above them.

The System's Roots in Financial Control

At its core, the court system is a financial institution, concerned with one thing: control over the financial resources of the people. The court serves as the mechanism by which wealth is redistributed from the individual to the state and corporations. When individuals fail to comply with the demands of the state—whether through taxes, fines, or fees—they are punished through the judicial system, their rights and property seized to satisfy the demands of the system.

The same goes for the enforcement of corporate policies by local law enforcement. The police are not primarily concerned with crime prevention or protection but are tasked with ensuring the population's compliance with corporate policies. This includes everything from issuing traffic tickets to arresting individuals who resist government control. These "policy enforcers" are part of the larger mechanism of control that operates under maritime law, which treats people as cargo rather than sovereign beings.

The people are conditioned to accept this treatment as normal, believing that they are being protected by the very system that is actually oppressing them. They are taught to fear authority and comply with arbitrary rules, and any attempt to resist is painted as a threat to the fabric of society.

The True Nature of Policing

In reality, the police are not peacekeepers. They are enforcement agents for the corporate state, tasked with extracting compliance and wealth from the public. Every ticket issued, every arrest made for victimless crimes, is not an act of justice but an act of extortion. It is a way to force the population to generate income for the state.

In many instances, police officers are no more than pawns in a larger game. They are conditioned to believe they are serving justice, while in reality, they are protecting the interests of a corrupt system. This extends to traffic enforcement, where the goal is not to keep the streets safe but to create a stream of revenue through fines. These revenue-generating operations are justified under the guise of "safety" or "law enforcement," but in truth, they serve only to fill the coffers of the state and corporations.

The illusion of justice extends even to the legal definitions of common terms. Words like "crime," "justice," and "law" are redefined through tools like Black's Law Dictionary to fit the needs of the corporate state. The truth is hidden behind a veil of language designed to confuse, intimidate, and disempower the people.

Resistance through Knowledge

The key to fighting back against this corrupt system lies in knowledge. The people must understand that they are not citizens of a free nation—they are assets of a corporate entity that exists to extract value from them. Understanding this, and taking action against the system, is the first step toward reclaiming sovereignty.

The attack on court officials' bonds, the exposure of the police's true role as policy enforcers, and the legal tools available to individuals to fight back are all ways to disrupt the corporate state's grip on power. The more people become aware of the truth—the more they question the legitimacy of the system—the closer they come to breaking the chains of control that have been wrapped around their lives.

The Network Awakens

Jackson's footsteps echoed in the quiet of his cramped apartment. He closed the door behind him, drawing the bolt shut before switching on a single dim light. The place was modest—nothing more than a studio with bare essentials. But it served its purpose: to keep him off the grid and out of sight.

The weight of the flash drive in his pocket felt heavier than before. He pulled it out and stared at it, the small metallic object holding the potential to upend everything. It was his key to the truth, to expose the system that bled the people dry and enslaved them in their own lives. But he couldn't do it alone.

Sliding the drive into his laptop, Jackson initiated the file decryption. Lines of code scrolled across the screen as his mind churned with what he'd just discovered. Taxes upon taxes, each designed to strip citizens of their hard-earned money, to reduce them to little more than cogs in a machine that produced wealth only for the few at the top. It was nothing short of a financial stranglehold, an engineered system of control that extended to every corner of life.

The file finished decrypting. Jackson's eyes narrowed as a series of names, addresses, and transaction logs appeared. It was a list of government officials, high-ranking corporate executives, and a web of interconnected shell companies used to launder money out of sight. They were siphoning funds directly from the public's contributions, hiding their wealth through loopholes and secret channels invisible to the average citizen.

"Bastards," he muttered, scrolling through the logs. Billions—no, trillions—were being funneled into private accounts while the people were told to tighten their belts, pay their dues, and remain obedient. It wasn't just robbery. It was an entire nation held hostage.

But then his gaze fell on another folder, labeled simply: Public Manipulation – Priority Targets. He hesitated, then opened it. Inside were files for key figures across various industries—actors, musicians, athletes—public figures who had been brought into the fold, knowingly or not. Their job? To distract. To entertain. To keep the people's eyes fixed on anything but the truth.

Jackson leaned back in his chair, staring at the screen. He understood now. This was why the games, the concerts, the endless stream of entertainment mattered so much. These celebrities weren't just performers—they were agents of distraction. Tools of control. And they were paid handsomely to keep the public's focus away from the oppressive system strangling them.

His fingers drummed against the desk as the pieces started to fall into place. If he wanted to fight back, he'd need to turn that same system against itself. He needed to find the people who could wake up the masses—the few voices strong enough to cut through the noise and expose what was really going on.

The phone on his desk buzzed, snapping him out of his thoughts. Another message from Specter.

"We're not alone. There are others. Meet us at Safehouse 12 tomorrow night. Midnight."

Jackson stared at the message for a moment, then typed back a single word: Confirmed.

He needed to know who these others were. He needed allies in this war against an invisible enemy. Standing up from his chair, Jackson moved to a small closet in the corner of the room. Pulling back the false wall, he revealed a secure safe embedded in the concrete. With a series of clicks, he opened it, revealing an assortment of IDs, burner phones, and cash.

He grabbed what he needed and then paused, his gaze falling on a faded photograph pinned to the back of the safe. It was old, a snapshot of a life that felt like it belonged to someone else. A smiling woman with auburn hair, laughing as a younger Jackson looked on with a grin. His sister. She had been the one to show him the truth. The one to first question the system. And the one to pay the price.

"Caroline..." Jackson whispered; his voice tight. He'd lost her to the machine. It was a debt he intended to collect, no matter the cost.

Slipping the essentials into his jacket, Jackson took a deep breath and left the apartment. He had a long night ahead of him, and it was just the beginning.

The city streets were nearly deserted by the time Jackson arrived at the designated address. Safehouse 12 looked like any other run-down building on the outskirts—a decrepit warehouse with boarded-up windows and faded graffiti on the walls. But appearances were deceiving. He approached the side entrance, knocking twice, pausing, and then knocking three more times in rapid succession.

The door creaked open, and a pair of wary eyes peered out. After a moment of scrutiny, the figure stepped back, allowing Jackson to enter. He was led through a series of dimly lit corridors, the air thick with the scent of old machinery and dust.

Finally, they reached a small room at the center of the building. A dozen people were gathered around a table, their faces tense, eyes sharp with a mix of fear and determination. Some looked like they belonged there—strong, battle-hardened types who had seen their share of conflict. Others seemed out of place: a middle-aged woman in a business suit, a young man with an artist's satchel slung over his shoulder, and an elderly man who looked like he hadn't slept in days.

"You made it," Specter's voice said from behind him. Jackson turned to see the hooded figure emerge from the shadows. "Wouldn't miss it," Jackson replied, stepping forward. "You said there were others. What's the plan?"

Specter motioned to the group. "We're the start. There are more like us—people who see the truth, who know the system is rigged and refuse to play by its rules. The trick is finding them and bringing them together. That's what tonight's about."

A murmur of agreement swept through the room. The woman in the business suit stood up, adjusting her glasses.

"We need to hit them where it hurts. Disrupt the flow of money. Expose the corruption. We've been taxed, monitored, and controlled from every angle. It's time we take back what's ours."

The elderly man nodded slowly. "The government has turned us into slaves—forced labor for a system that benefits no one but those at the top. But if we can sever the chains, show people what's really happening..."

"Then we might stand a chance," Jackson finished for him, meeting Specter's gaze. "I've seen the files. I know what we're up against."

"Good," Specter said softly. "Then you know it's not just about survival. It's about reclaiming our freedom. Tonight, we start planning our first strike. One that'll make them sit up and pay attention."

Jackson took a seat at the table, the weight of his resolve settling around him like armor. The road ahead would be dangerous. People would get hurt. Some might even die. But there was no turning back now. They were fighting for something far greater than themselves.

And for the first time, Jackson felt a spark of hope.

Because now, he wasn't alone.

The Hidden Trust and the Role of the Federal Reserve

The Creation of the Trust at Birth

From the very moment a child is born in the United States, the system begins to operate behind the scenes, unbeknownst to the child or the parents. A hidden financial system comes into play—one that starts when the birth certificate is signed and registered. The signing of this certificate does not merely acknowledge the child's existence but creates a legal entity—a "legal fiction." This entity, named after the child, is not a living person, but a vessel for the state.

What most people do not realize is that with the registration of their birth, the United States government begins a financial transaction on their behalf, using the child's Social Security number as a key identifier. This Social Security number is not just a tool for taxation or public services; it is tied directly to a financial trust account. When a child is born, $1 million is allegedly placed into this account, though the money does not exist in the traditional sense. The money is created in the form of a loan or credit, which builds interest over time, all of which stays in the hands of the Federal Reserve and private financial entities.

This money, while appearing to be an asset for the individual, remains inaccessible to them. By the time a person reaches adulthood, the balance in the account could theoretically amount to millions of dollars, but the individual has no direct access to it. This is the hidden truth behind the financial system in the United States: people are born with a trust account they can never touch, and the wealth built in these accounts flows into the corporate state, not the people.

The Federal Reserve: Controlling the People's Wealth The Federal Reserve, which operates as a private

institution despite being considered the central banking system of the U.S., is at the heart of this financial scheme. The true role of the Federal Reserve is to manage and control the financial assets tied to the Social Security numbers of every American citizen. These accounts, which are hidden in plain sight, are used as collateral to fund loans, issue currency, and generate wealth for the banks and corporations that control the system. The Federal Reserve is the central player in maintaining this wealth, but they operate in secrecy, ensuring that the public remains unaware of the funds that have been earmarked for them.

The accounts created at birth are theoretically worth millions by the time a person reaches 18 years old, but these funds are not accessible by the individual. Instead, the wealth is siphoned off by the Federal Reserve, used to control the market, manipulate the financial system, and fund government operations. People are told that they are free citizens with rights to their wealth, but in truth, their financial freedom is nothing more than an illusion.

The Role of the Federal Judge as Trustee

When you step into a courtroom, you are not simply facing a judge as an impartial administrator of justice. You are dealing with a federal trustee, whose primary role is not to serve justice but to manage the trust accounts tied to each person's Social Security number. The judge is the fiduciary of these accounts, responsible for ensuring that the trust funds are managed according to the rules set forth by the Federal Reserve. The judge's role in the courtroom is not to dispense justice for the people but to protect the corporate interests of the system.

The true power of the judge is in their ability to access and control these hidden accounts. Though the public is never informed about the existence of these trust accounts or the vast wealth they supposedly contain, the judge holds the keys to this system, dictating who has access to the funds and how they are distributed. The courts, rather than providing true justice, serve to maintain the illusion of freedom while ensuring that the financial system remains in the hands of the powerful.

Legal Fiction and the Birth Certificate

The concept of "legal fiction" is central to understanding the system that controls the lives of American citizens. A birth certificate, which is meant to acknowledge the birth of a child, is actually the creation of a legal entity—a fictitious person—under the control of the state. The moment a birth certificate is signed, the individual ceases to exist as a sovereign being and is instead categorized as "property" of the state. This entity is subject to the laws of the state, and its name is used to generate wealth for the government and private corporations. The birth certificate, in this sense, is the starting point for a financial system that treats citizens as collateral for loans and debt.

Furthermore, when the parents sign the birth certificate, they are unknowingly entering into a contract with the state. This contract places their child under the jurisdiction of corporate law, rather than common law. The child's name, which is now a legal fiction, is used to fund the creation of the financial accounts within the Federal Reserve system. These accounts are tied to the child's Social Security number and used as collateral for loans, bond issues, and other financial transactions that benefit the state and private banks.

The Social Security Number and the Hidden Trust

The Social Security number (SSN) is not just a tool for the government to track its citizens; it is, in fact, a financial identifier that links individuals to this hidden trust system. Each person's SSN is directly tied to a trust account created for them at birth. This account is managed by the Federal Reserve and is used as collateral in the global financial system.

The SSN on the back of every Social Security card is not simply a number—it's a key to a vault of hidden wealth. This trust account theoretically holds millions of dollars, accumulating wealth in the form of interest over time. However, this money does not belong to the individual. It is controlled by the Federal Reserve and other financial institutions, and the individual has no access to it. The true value of the account is never disclosed to the individual, and they are kept in the dark about its existence.

The Illusion of Financial Freedom

Despite the wealth theoretically available to them, the individual has no access to their trust account. The money generated from these accounts is not for the people—it is for the system. While individuals are led to believe that they have rights to their property and financial freedom, in reality, they are trapped in a system where their wealth is used for the benefit of the state and corporate interests. This hidden system of financial manipulation keeps the masses in a state of ignorance, unable to access the wealth that has been created in their name.

This wealth, theoretically, exists only on paper and is used to fund government operations, pay off corporate debts, and further enrich those who control the system. The individual is left out, with no ability to access their wealth or change their circumstances. The reality of the system is that the people are not free; they are subjects of a financial empire that uses their names and Social Security numbers to build wealth for the elites.

The Police: Enforcers of the System

The police, often seen as protectors of the public, are in fact enforcers of a system designed to keep the population under control. The very name "police" is derived from the word "policy," indicating that their role is to enforce the policies of the state. They are not there to protect the rights of the people but to ensure that the corporate interests of the state are maintained.

In practice, this means that police officers are often tasked with extorting money from the population, whether through fines, tickets, or other means. They act as agents of the state, carrying out their duties without understanding the true nature of the system they are supporting. These individuals, many of whom are unaware of the bigger picture, are caught in a system of control, just like the rest of the population.

Suing the Court and Attacking Bonds

One of the little-known facts about the legal system is that anyone can challenge the actions of those in power, including members of the court. The concept of "attacking the bond" refers to the ability to sue members of the court—judges, lawyers, and even police officers—for their actions, based on the financial bonds that are attached to their position. These bonds serve as a form of collateral to protect the public from misconduct, and they can be targeted in legal actions.

The fact that people can challenge the bonds of these public officials is rarely spoken of, but it is an important tool for reclaiming power. It serves as a reminder that the people are not powerless in the face of this system. By holding these individuals accountable, citizens can begin to dismantle the facade of legal authority and expose the corruption that underlies the system.

The First Strike

The tension in the room was palpable as Jackson surveyed the faces around the table. Everyone was there because they shared a mission—to dismantle the shackles that bound them all to a system of corruption.

Specter stood at the head of the table, pointing to a map sprawled across its surface. Markers littered the map, pinpointing government buildings, corporate headquarters, and popular entertainment venues. "Our first target is a gala at the city's convention center next week," Specter announced, tracing his finger to the largest marker. "It's a gathering for the city's elite—a celebration of their wealth, power, and, ultimately, their corruption."

Jackson leaned in, focused. "What's the plan?"

The businesswoman adjusted her glasses, her expression all business. "Insider info suggests a large cash transfer will happen during the event. If we can intercept it—or even just expose it—we'll send a powerful message: their control isn't invincible."

Jackson nodded thoughtfully. "We can't just walk in and take it. How do we pull this off?"

"Exactly," Specter replied, his eyes narrowing with determination. "We'll need a distraction to draw attention away from the transfer. Meanwhile, we leak enough information to get the public's attention. Everyone has a role."

An elderly man at the table leaned forward. "I can set up a small fireworks display outside, something to draw eyes away from the inside. Just enough to cause a commotion."

The artist joined in, his face lighting up. "I'll create posters, flyers—something bold to make people question what's really happening. We get the word out right, and we'll have everyone talking."

The businesswoman nodded. "I've got media contacts who can amplify the story. If we play our cards right, the truth will spread fast."

Jackson felt a surge of adrenaline as the plan took shape. "Timing is everything. The transfer is the core, but we need everyone watching us when it goes down."

Specter gave an approving nod, a glint of excitement breaking his usual stern demeanor. "Exactly. We're not just going to disrupt this event; we're going to shake the whole network. Let's show them that we're not powerless. This is the first strike."

As the group brainstormed into the night, Jackson could feel the weight of their mission settle on his shoulders. This wasn't just one attack; it was the start of a movement, one meant to spark an awakening in people numbed by endless entertainment and consumerism.

The night of the gala arrived, and Jackson slipped into a simple black suit that would help him blend with the crowd. He took a steadying breath as he approached the glittering convention center, which buzzed with laughter and music. But Jackson knew the ugly truth hidden behind the glitz—the greed, deception, and manipulation fueling it all.

He spotted the businesswoman coordinating the operation through her headset. She waved him over. "Everything's set. The fireworks start at eight sharp, right before the transfer begins."

Jackson nodded. "Where's the transfer happening?"

"Downstairs, in a secure vault. Heavily guarded," she replied, indicating a stairwell leading down. "You'll need a distraction."

Jackson made his way to a side door where the elderly man waited, a box of fireworks clutched in his hands. "You ready for this?" Jackson asked.

The man nodded, determined. "Once this goes off, you'll have your opening."

Jackson found his spot near the entrance, breathing in deeply as he listened to the sounds of the gala—the music, laughter, and clinking glasses, all a thin veneer over deep-seated corruption. It only fueled his resolve.

At exactly eight, fireworks exploded outside, a dazzling display that immediately drew the crowd's attention. As gasps and murmurs filled the room, Jackson slipped into the shadows.

"Now!" he urged the elderly man forward. The crackling display above created enough chaos to pull the guards outside, leaving Jackson a path down to the vault.

Navigating through dimly lit hallways, Jackson moved swiftly, the sounds of the gala fading as he descended. He reached the vault door, where two guards remained vigilant, unaware of the chaos outside.

Jackson whispered to the elderly man beside him, "Can you handle them?"

With a resolute nod, the man approached, stumbling as he collided with one guard. In the confusion, he used swift, unexpected moves to incapacitate both guards before they knew what hit them.

"Let's go," Jackson murmured, pulling out a makeshift device to override the vault's electronic lock. As the mechanism whirred, Jackson felt the pressure of time like a weight on his shoulders. Failure wasn't an option.

The lock clicked, and the door swung open. Inside, stacks of cash and documents lay in organized rows. Jackson quickly grabbed several bundles of cash and snapped photos of the incriminating documents with his phone. "This is going to blow everything wide open," he whispered.

Just then, footsteps echoed down the hallway. Alarms began blaring, cutting through the silence. "We need to move!" he shouted, grabbing what he could before dashing back toward the exit.

They sprinted up the stairs, adrenaline surging through them as the faint sound of pursuit grew louder. Guards, now alerted, converged behind them. "Stop!" a voice shouted, but Jackson and the elderly man bolted forward, unyielding.

Bursting outside, they were met by the remnants of the fireworks display, still capturing the crowd's gaze. Jackson scanned the area until he spotted the others waiting in a nearby alley.

“There!” the elderly man pointed as they sprinted toward safety, their pursuers on their heels.

They reached the alley where the businesswoman and artist waited, breathless and anxious. “Did you get it?” the businesswoman asked, excitement glinting in her eyes.

Jackson held up the cash and documents triumphantly. “We have everything we need. Let’s show the world what they’re hiding.”

Together, they melted into the shadows, carrying with them the truth that would soon shake the city to its core.

The Implant

Jackson Rivers sat in the quiet, dimly lit room, his mind racing. The news reports had been unsettling—Neurolink, Elon's brain implant company, had successfully launched human trials. The implants were intended to help paralyzed individuals regain movement, but Jackson had heard the whispers of darker possibilities. The technology, designed to let people control devices with their minds, could also be weaponized. The implants could control more than movement—they could control thoughts, actions, and, worst of all, freedom.

Elon's latest breakthrough had combined the implant with RNA technology. The consequences were chilling: once embedded, these implants could connect directly to the neural pathways in a way that allowed external manipulation. Jackson shuddered at the thought. People would lose their autonomy, becoming puppets at the mercy of those who controlled the technology. It wasn't just about healing anymore; it was about control.

Across the world, the trials were underway, and some subjects were already reporting strange experiences. One, a man who had been paralyzed for years, described the feeling of his body reacting faster than he could think. A sense of losing himself, his very will, to the device that was supposed to restore him. This wasn't recovery; it was transformation—into something far darker.

Then there was the disturbing story of a man in a wheelchair, playing video games at what seemed like a normal pace. But his expressions were blank, mechanical. When he spoke, his words seemed rehearsed, almost as though the implant was reading his mind faster than he could comprehend, pushing him to act, to speak. The world didn't know the full truth yet, but Jackson could feel the gears turning in his mind. This was the beginning of something catastrophic. It almost seemed like the creation of something out of a nightmare—like the rise of the machines from the Terminator films. What if this was how it all started? What if this technology wasn't just a tool for healing, but the precursor to a world where machines controlled the very people who created them?

He would not let this happen. Not to him, not to anyone.

Jackson's heart pounded as he leaned forward, staring at the glowing screen in front of him. The implant could lodge itself deep into the brain, interfacing with neurons, becoming part of the person. The more it connected, the more control it gained, until one day, the person might wake up and realize that they had no control left at all.

His fingers curled into fists. He knew it wasn't just technology anymore—it was a weapon. And it wasn't just Elon at the helm. Governments, corporations, and shadowy figures stood ready to exploit the technology for their own gain. The last bastion of human freedom would be crushed under the weight of this new order.

But Jackson would not be a pawn. He had seen enough, learned enough, to know that there was always a way to fight back. He'd make sure this technology was never used to strip away a person's humanity. The fight for freedom, for control over one's own body and mind, had just begun.

And Jackson Rivers was ready to lead it.

Exposure and Retribution

The safehouse hummed with urgency. Jackson stood at the center of a cluttered table, surrounded by resistance members who pored over the files he had just retrieved from the government's vault. Every document revealed layers of corruption, deception, and manipulation—the depth of which made Jackson's stomach twist. It was as if they had been playing a game of monopoly, with the people as the pawns, their lives controlled by a corrupt system designed to siphon their resources through endless taxes and backdoor deals.

Claire, the businesswoman, studied a set of receipts in disbelief. "It's worse than we imagined," she whispered. "Hidden taxes on everything—utilities, food, even medical expenses. They've devised a system that bleeds us dry in ways we never even considered."

Jackson nodded. "They've built a facade of freedom, but in truth, we're nothing more than slaves. It's just a game to them. A game they've rigged to extract from us at every turn."

"Slaves who are waking up," Specter, the shadowy leader, said, stepping forward with a document in hand. "This right here—a hidden tax amendment buried deep in the legal code—shows how they've used legal loopholes to impose fees on necessities and funnel the money into private accounts. This isn't just taxation, it's financial enslavement."

Jackson clenched his fists. "They've stripped us of everything we own and now, with our own money, they keep us under control. They've hidden it all behind legal jargon and complicated codes no one ever bothers to read. But we've read it."

Claire's voice grew firm. "And now, we make sure everyone else reads it too."

A plan took shape quickly. The documents would be leaked to every independent journalist, every media outlet, and whistleblower network they could find. The mainstream media might be bought and paid for, but there were still those out there who would risk everything to reveal the truth.

"We need to prepare for the backlash," Jackson warned, glancing at Specter. "They won't just let this slide."

Specter's eyes hardened. "The moment we exposed them, we became targets. But we have no choice now. It's not just about us. It's about everyone who's been enslaved."

"Then we hit them harder," Jackson replied, the determination in his voice unwavering. "More leaks. More secrets. We make it impossible for them to sweep this under the rug."

Claire nodded. "First, though, we secure our safehouses.

If they find us…"

"They won't," Specter interjected, cutting her off. "We've made contingency plans. Our people have already moved to safer locations. But we have to be careful. Every move has to be calculated."

Jackson's jaw tightened. "Let's get to work. The world needs to know the truth."

At midnight, the leak went live. Jackson watched as article after article appeared online, each one uncovering another layer of the government's financial deceit. Videos of intercepted calls, photos of illegal transactions, memos between high-ranking officials—all of it was laid bare for the world to see.

Within hours, the internet exploded. Social media was ablaze with outrage. Hashtags like #TaxSlavery and #EndTheCorruption began trending worldwide. People who had never questioned the system were suddenly seeing the truth. They'd been deceived. They'd been exploited.

"We did it," Claire breathed, her eyes wide with disbelief. "They're seeing it now. They can't deny it anymore."

Jackson allowed himself a small smile. The fight wasn't over, but this moment felt like a victory. "This is just the beginning. They'll try to bury us. Discredit us. Destroy us. But we're ready."

"We've got more," Specter said, crossing his arms. "More documents. More evidence. We keep exposing them, piece by piece. We make them accountable for every crime they've committed."

But even as Jackson agreed, a cold feeling settled in his chest. He had seen the lengths the government would go to protect its secrets. He had witnessed firsthand the lengths they would go to silence those who posed a threat. And now, they were coming for him.

"Stay vigilant," Jackson warned. His eyes swept the room, locking with every pair of eyes around him. "We can't afford to drop our guard. Not even for a second."

The resistance members nodded in agreement. They knew what was at stake. They were all in this together, their lives bound by a common purpose: to expose the truth and free the people from the shackles of government oppression.

The backlash came fast and furious. Within hours, government officials were on every major news outlet, dismissing the documents as forgeries and branding the resistance as terrorists. The mainstream media spun the narrative, painting the resistance as radical extremists bent on destabilizing the nation.

But the truth had already taken root. Protests erupted across the country. Citizens took to the streets, demanding answers. The government scrambled to contain the unrest, deploying riot police and cutting off internet access in several regions.

Jackson watched the chaos unfold on a small TV in the corner of the safehouse. The people were awake now. They were questioning everything. But the government's response was more brutal than he'd anticipated.

"We need to go underground," Specter said, his voice tense. "They've deployed drones. They've got facial recognition. They're coming for us."

"Then we disappear," Jackson said, his voice resolute. "We switch locations. Change our identities. Keep pushing the truth. We can't stop now."

But even as he spoke, a chilling thought crossed his mind. He knew they were walking a razor's edge. One wrong move, and everything would come crashing down. But they had no choice. Not when the alternative was to let the system keep its chokehold on the people.

Later that night, as Jackson sat alone in the darkness, his laptop flickering in front of him, his mind raced. Plans, contingencies, the faces of those he had lost, and the faces of those who had stood with him. He couldn't let them down. Not now.

Then a message appeared on his screen—a single line that made his blood run cold:

"They know who you are. Leave now. – S."

Jackson slammed the laptop shut. Without a word, he bolted from his chair, alerting the others. "We're compromised. We need to move. Now."

Panic surged through the group, but they reacted with the precision of those who had already been through hell. Within minutes, they gathered their things and rushed toward the exits.

Jackson glanced back one last time at the safehouse—his home, for the moment—and then stepped into the cold night. The government would be looking for them. They would be hunted. But Jackson knew one thing for sure:

They could try to erase him. But they couldn't erase the truth.

And that truth, no matter how hard they fought to bury it, was what would set them—and everyone else—free.

Escaping the Grid

The night was pitch black as Jackson and the others raced through the backstreets of the city, their breaths visible in the crisp air. Every shadow seemed to conceal a threat, every passing car a potential danger. They moved quickly, blending into the alleyways and abandoned buildings, keeping to the path Specter had mapped out earlier.

"Keep moving!" Specter urged, his voice low but forceful. He glanced over his shoulder, scanning for any signs of pursuit. "We can't afford to slow down now."

Jackson nodded, his senses on high alert. The encrypted message warning them to leave hadn't given them much time, but it had been enough to make a hasty escape. Whoever had sent it—whether it was an ally within the system or someone else—had saved them for now.

"What's the plan?" Claire whispered, her eyes darting nervously around. "We can't keep running forever."

"We're not running," Jackson replied, his gaze hard. "We're repositioning."

Specter flashed him a brief grin. "I like the sound of that."

They reached an abandoned subway tunnel and ducked inside, the darkness swallowing them whole. The air was musty, and the sound of dripping water echoed off the walls. Jackson slowed his pace, allowing everyone to catch their breath.

"We have safe houses spread throughout the city," Specter explained quietly. "But we need to be smart. If they've compromised this one, there's no telling how many others they might know about."

"Then we'll have to create new ones," Jackson said, thinking quickly. "We can't rely on anything static. We need to stay mobile—use temporary shelters, keep changing locations."

Claire frowned. "How do we coordinate if we're constantly on the move?"

"I've got an idea," Jackson replied, reaching into his bag and pulling out a small device. "It's a signal scrambler I've been working on. It'll block surveillance drones from tracking us by disrupting their signal. We use it to move in and out of an area without being detected."

Specter raised an eyebrow. "You built this yourself?"

Jackson shrugged. "I had some help. But it's untraceable, and it should buy us some time."

"Then let's put it to good use," Specter said. He glanced at the others, who were watching the exchange with a mix of fear and anticipation. "We need to split up. Small groups. It'll make us harder to track."

Jackson agreed, turning to Claire and the elderly man. "You two go together. Head to the old industrial district on the east side—it's mostly abandoned, and there are some places there we can use as temporary bases."

The elderly man nodded; his expression grim but resolute. "We'll be careful."

"Specter and I will go south," Jackson continued. "There's an underground network we can use to stay off the grid. We'll set up a new communications hub and reach out to our contacts."

Claire looked at him, worry etched on her face. "What if they catch you?"

"They won't," Jackson said firmly. "We'll keep moving. Stay low, keep quiet, and don't use any electronics unless you're certain it's secure."

She hesitated, then nodded. "Good luck." "Same to you."

With that, they split off into the darkness, disappearing into the night like ghosts. Jackson kept his head down, his mind racing as he and Specter made their way south. The weight of their mission pressed heavily on him, but he pushed it aside, focusing on the task at hand.

"Think they'll make it?" Specter asked quietly as they moved through the shadows.

"They have to," Jackson replied. "We're all each other's got now."

Specter fell silent, and they continued in tense silence, slipping through back alleys and deserted streets until they reached the entrance to an old maintenance tunnel. Jackson knelt down, using a small tool to pry open the rusted grate.

"After you," he said, gesturing for Specter to go first.

Specter glanced at him, then slid into the tunnel, his silhouette disappearing into the darkness. Jackson followed, pulling the grate back into place behind them. The tunnel was narrow and damp, the air thick with the scent of decay. They moved carefully, their footsteps echoing softly.

After what felt like an eternity, they emerged into a larger underground chamber. It was an old storage facility, long abandoned and forgotten. Jackson glanced around, assessing the space.

"This will work," he said. "We can set up here, at least for a while."

Specter nodded; his expression thoughtful. "What's the next move, then?"

Jackson took a deep breath. "We need to find out how they tracked us. There's a mole, or they've developed new tech that can bypass our security measures. Either way, we're vulnerable."

"Agreed," Specter said. "But we also need to keep the pressure on. The public is still riled up from the leaks. If we disappear now, it'll be too easy for the government to reassert control."

"Then we keep hitting them with more," Jackson said, a determined glint in his eye. "More leaks, more disruptions, anything to keep them off balance."

Specter grinned. "I like the way you think."

They spent the next several hours setting up a makeshift base, using old equipment Specter had stashed in the tunnels years ago. It wasn't much, but it was enough to get them back online and reconnect with the others.

As Jackson worked, his mind kept drifting back to the message that had warned them to leave. Who had sent it? And how had they known the government was closing in?

"We have to find out who tipped us off," he muttered, half to himself.

Specter glanced over. "You think it's someone on the inside?"

"Maybe," Jackson replied. "Or it could be a trap. They might be trying to draw us out, get us to expose ourselves."

"Then we play it smart," Specter said, his tone serious. "We move carefully and verify everything twice. No risks, no assumptions."

Jackson nodded, but he couldn't shake the feeling that they were already one step behind. Whoever was hunting them, whoever had betrayed them—it was only a matter of time before they caught up.

And when they did, Jackson knew they'd have to be ready to fight back.

The next day, as dawn broke over the city, Jackson received another message on his encrypted device. It was short, just a few words, but it sent a chill down his spine:

"The chains tighten. Be ready. – S."

He showed it to Specter, who frowned. "They're closing in."

Jackson nodded grimly. "But so are we."

They were playing a dangerous game, a cat-and-mouse chase through the shadows. But Jackson was determined. They wouldn't go down without a fight.

Not until every citizen was free.

The Real Terrorists

Jackson seethed as he watched the speeches from the elites of the United Nations. Behind their polished facades and smooth words, they were plotting something far darker than just a global alliance. They were orchestrating the rise of a one-world government—one where they sat at the top, their wealth and power unchallenged. The rest of the world? Just cogs in their grand machine, helpless to fight back.

The people on the streets, those fighting for survival, those calling for justice, weren't the terrorists. It was these men and women—the ones in their ivory towers, cloaked in wealth and privilege. They had long ago decided that the world was theirs to control, and anyone who threatened their grip on power was a threat to be crushed. Their strategies were simple: divide, conquer, and control.

Jackson's eyes narrowed. The more he saw of their grand plan, the clearer it became: these weren't the leaders of a peaceful world, they were the architects of a global dictatorship. And Jackson couldn't let that happen. He couldn't sit back and watch as these rich, powerful elites turned the world into their personal playground. No, they were the real terrorists—using fear, manipulation, and surveillance as weapons to strip humanity of its freedom. They deserved to be eradicated, not feared.

The thought fueled his fire. He wasn't going to wait for them to come for him. He was going to take the fight to them. He would expose their corruption, turn their own system against them, and make them run.

These so-called rulers needed to be shown they were no longer safe, no longer untouchable. It was time for the world to realize the truth. The time for revolution was now. And Jackson Rivers would lead the charge. The elites wouldn't see it coming.

Poison on the Plate

The morning sun filtered weakly through the window as Jackson sat at the kitchen table of the safe house, his mind still reeling from the events of the previous night. The others were resting, catching whatever sleep they could. But Jackson couldn't sleep, not after what he'd learned.

He absently poured a bowl of cereal and sat down, staring blankly at the colorful box in front of him. The familiar brand logo seemed almost comforting in its normalcy. But then, as he took a closer look at the ingredients list, something caught his eye. A long, chemical name he couldn't immediately recognize.

"What the...?" he muttered, leaning in closer. His eyes scanned the fine print, and as he read more, a horrifying realization began to dawn on him. He dropped his spoon and grabbed his laptop, furiously typing in the chemical names from the cereal box.

The results sent a chill down his spine.

"Pesticides... neurotoxins... carcinogens..." he whispered, his voice trailing off as the pieces began to fall into place. "They're not even hiding it."

He pushed the cereal bowl away, his appetite completely gone. The box, which had seemed so innocent a moment ago, now looked like a murder weapon in his hands. These weren't food additives—they were poisons. Substances designed to keep people docile, mentally impaired, and sick.

With a sudden surge of anger, Jackson stood up, knocking the chair back. He grabbed the box and threw it into the trash, his mind racing.

"This is why they've been going after farmers," he said to himself, pacing the small kitchen. "It's not just about corporate control. They want to eliminate any source of natural, uncontaminated food. They're shutting down family farms, forcing people to buy from government-controlled suppliers. The food supply… they want to control every bite we eat."

He recalled the recent news reports—government raids on local farms and new regulations making it nearly impossible for independent growers to operate. They'd said it was about safety, about efficiency. But Jackson knew better now.

"They want to keep us stupid," he whispered, clenching his fists. "If you control the food, you control the people. If you poison the food, you poison the people."

The words echoed in his mind like a mantra. Control. Poison. Eliminate.

Just then, the faint hum of an aircraft reverberated through the walls, drawing Jackson's attention. He moved quickly to the window and looked up. A large plane was flying low overhead, crisscrossing the sky with long, thick trails of white mist. Jackson's eyes widened as he watched, realization dawning.

"Chemtrails…" he muttered. "They're spraying… something."

He dashed back to his laptop, pulling up satellite images and flight patterns. The data was overwhelming. Planes crisscrossed not just his city but the entire country, laying down a fine layer of chemicals—poisons that would settle over fields, water supplies, and homes.

A sudden broadcast interruption on his laptop's screen made him freeze. The image shifted to a government press conference, a suited official standing behind a podium with a grave expression on his face.

"Due to recent weather anomalies, we're implementing emergency climate measures to protect our environment and population. This is part of our ongoing strategy to combat the harmful effects of climate change. We ask for your cooperation in these difficult times..."

Jackson's heart pounded. Climate change? That's what they were calling this? It was the perfect cover. No one would question emergency measures for the sake of the planet. No one would look too closely at what was in those planes.

But Jackson knew. He knew now.

"It's not about climate change," he whispered, his voice trembling with rage. "They're killing us. Slowly. They've been doing it for years—right under our noses."

He turned back to his laptop, pulling up old documents, research papers, and anything he could find. The deeper he dug, the more horrifying the picture became. The chemicals in the food, the poisons in the water, the pollutants in the air—all part of a massive, coordinated effort to weaken the population. And it wasn't just about making people sick or stupid. It was about control. About ensuring that anyone who did wake up to the truth was too weakened to fight back.

His fingers flew across the keyboard, searching for any mention of these plans. He stumbled upon a series of leaked memos—cryptic references to "population management" and "resource allocation." One phrase stood out, sending a shiver down his spine:

"Reduction of non-essential personnel."

"They're treating us like livestock," Jackson said, his voice shaking with anger. "Cull the herd, keep the numbers down. They don't see us as people. They see us as a problem to be managed. Too many mouths to feed, too many voices to silence. The only solution they see is elimination."

His thoughts were interrupted by another broadcast, this one from a different channel. An independent journalist broadcasting from what looked like a small, hidden studio.

"Reports are coming in that family farms across the Midwest are being shut down under the guise of environmental protection," the journalist said, her voice tense. "But sources on the ground tell a different story—fields are being confiscated, crops burned, and anyone who resists is being silenced. It's clear that this has nothing to do with climate change. This is about control. About consolidating the food supply into the hands of a few mega-corporations, all of whom are in bed with the government."

Jackson's grip tightened on the edge of the table. So, it's true.

He switched back to the satellite feed, watching as the plane's chemtrail spread across the sky. The realization hit him like a punch to the gut. This wasn't just about weakening the population. It was about something far worse.

"They want to kill us," he breathed. "Not just control—eliminate. Targeted extermination, slowly poisoning every man, woman, and child until we're too weak, too sick… or just gone."

He slumped back in his chair, his mind racing. This explained everything—the relentless push for government dependency, the censorship, the erosion of freedoms. It all led back to the same conclusion.

"They've declared war on us," he whispered. "And we didn't even know it."

But Jackson wasn't ready to surrender. If the government wanted a war, then they would get one.

"They want to kill us like insects? Then we need to cut off the head of the snake."

His mind whirred with plans and strategies. The time for half-measures was over. If they didn't act now, there wouldn't be a country left to save.

Jackson stood up, his resolve hardening. He reached for his weapon and strapped it on. Every man and woman who believed in freedom needed to hear this. They needed to know what was really happening—and why it was time to fight back.

"They've underestimated us," he said, his voice firm and steady. "They think we're stupid, weakened, too broken to resist. But they've forgotten one thing: we are the people. And when pushed too far, we will push back."

With one last glance at the poisoned sky outside, Jackson turned and left the safe house.

It was time to rally the resistance.

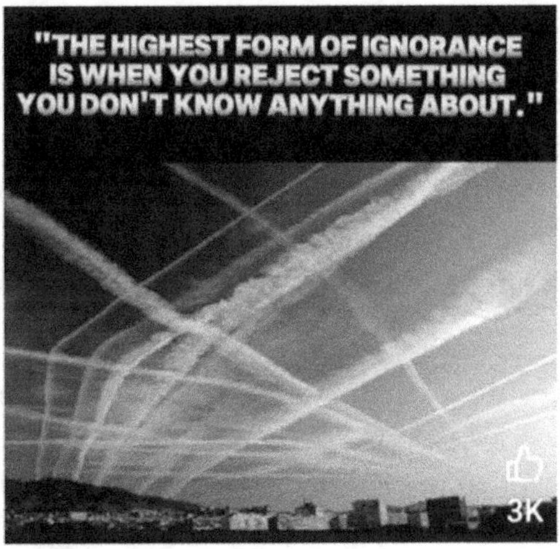
"THE HIGHEST FORM OF IGNORANCE IS WHEN YOU REJECT SOMETHING YOU DON'T KNOW ANYTHING ABOUT."
3K

Jackson's Address to the People

Jackson stood at the heart of the rally, facing the sea of people who had gathered to hear the truth. His voice was steady, but the fire within him burned through every word as he read aloud the message he had crafted. He knew this was more than just a speech—it was a declaration, a call to action.

"I am writing to express my deep concern and outrage over the actions of our government and certain powerful corporations that are deliberately endangering the lives of every man and woman in this country. The recent emergence of companies like Apeel, which claims to help food last longer, is just one example of how we are being systematically poisoned. The so-called protective compound used by Apeel is, in fact, a dangerous substance that cannot be removed from our food, posing a severe risk to public health.

This alarming situation is exacerbated by the involvement of figures like Bill Gates and corporations such as Microsoft. It is becoming increasingly clear that their motivations are far from altruistic. Instead of protecting the public, their actions suggest a concerted effort to depopulate the United States. The introduction of this compound in our food supply is just one part of a broader strategy to weaken and control the population.

Furthermore, I am deeply troubled by the evidence suggesting that Bill Gates and Microsoft are playing a significant role in simulating global warming through carbon dioxide levels. But the reality is, the carbon they speak of isn't the earth's atmosphere. It's the men and women they want to exterminate. Through the distribution of "forever chemicals" in our environment, they are releasing toxic substances into the air under the guise of environmental protection. But the true purpose is far darker: the systematic poisoning of our citizens.

The Federal Food and Drug Administration (FDA), an agency that should be safeguarding our health, has been compromised. Powerful corporate interests have usurped its authority, allowing them to carry out their harmful agenda unchecked. This betrayal of public trust is unacceptable.

I demand immediate action to investigate these serious allegations and hold accountable those responsible for poisoning our food and environment. We cannot allow our government and corporations to continue endangering the lives of American citizens for their own nefarious goals.

Additionally, it is becoming clear that figures like Bill Gates and corporations such as Microsoft are not just manipulating the food supply, but also simulating global warming by intentionally distributing toxic chemicals that pollute our air. These chemicals contain metals that can be absorbed through the skin, further compromising our health. Worse yet, these technologies are capable of using these metals as conductors to amplify harm. They are microwaving the population under the guise of environmental protection.

I urge you to stand with the people. We must protect our health, our environment, and our future. We cannot allow ourselves to be controlled and harmed by those who think they own us. We must demand transparency, accountability, and the preservation of our rights and well-being."

The crowd fell silent as Jackson's words sank in, the weight of the truth hitting harder than any blow. The time for standing back was over. The people were ready. It was time to fight.

The Sky's Secret

Jackson stepped outside the safehouse, his head still spinning with the newfound information. The cold morning air hit him like a slap, but he barely noticed. His eyes were fixed on the sky above, where a network of crisscrossing chemtrails lingered ominously, weaving a pale web of chemicals high above the land.

The sight was enough to make his stomach churn. They were everywhere—thin, white trails that spread like a net, coating the landscape. It wasn't until now that he truly understood their purpose.

"Forever chemicals," he whispered, the words bitter on his tongue. These compounds were designed to persist in the environment indefinitely, building up in the soil, water, and air. The media had spun it as a new environmental crisis—climate change gone awry. But Jackson could see the truth now.

The government wasn't reacting to climate change. They were creating it.

Everywhere he looked, there were signs of decay—crops failing, animals dying, regions turning to wasteland. Still, the planes flew overhead, day after day, spreading their toxic cargo like clockwork.

Jackson stepped further into the yard, the grass crunching beneath his boots. He glanced down and realized the blades were coated in a fine, powdery residue. Crouching, he ran his fingers over the brittle leaves, then lifted his hand to his nose. The faint, acrid scent made his eyes water.

"God," he muttered, wiping his hand on his jeans. "It's everywhere."

He turned slowly, eyes scanning the sky, the fields, the forest beyond. It felt like the world was suffocating under a blanket of poison. Yet, people were told it was for their own good.

"Climate change," he scoffed bitterly. "The perfect scapegoat, the perfect lie. They're simulating global warming to spread fear, using it as an excuse to dump chemicals on farmlands."

He saw it now—these chemicals were killing the soil, rendering it infertile, poisoning the crops, and driving farmers out of business. The government could then swoop in with "solutions" to control the food supply.

"They're eliminating the farmers," Jackson said, his voice rising with anger. "They want to control who eats and who doesn't. And it's not just the food—they're dumping this poison on us too."

He remembered the strange illnesses cropping up in his community—rashes, unexplained fatigue, neurological symptoms that no doctor could pinpoint. They'd blamed it on allergies, stress. But now, he knew better. The chemicals weren't just harming the land; they were poisoning the people too, seeping into their bodies with every breath.

"Forever chemicals," he repeated, shaking his head. "They're not just in the air. They're inside us."

He thought of a conversation with an old friend, a biochemist who had once worked for the government. She'd whispered about compounds that could subtly alter the body—disrupt hormones, weaken the immune system, even change how people thought and felt. At the time, he'd dismissed it as paranoia.

But standing here, breathing in the tainted air, he felt it. The heaviness in his chest, the metallic taste in his mouth, the sluggishness seeping into his muscles. It was real.

"It's been going on for a long time," he muttered, piecing it together. "They've been doing this for years. Slowly, methodically, poisoning us until we're too weak to resist, too broken to fight back."

A sudden noise caught his attention, and Jackson glanced up. Another plane, high above, cut across the sky, trailing its chemical stream. His anger flared. Every drop of poison was designed to manipulate and control.

"They want to eliminate us," he whispered, voice trembling with rage. "They see us as carbon—expendable. Too many people, too much 'carbon,' so they use this poison to thin us out. And all the while, they blame it on climate change."

He clenched his fists, nails digging into his palms. The government's propaganda machine was in full swing, pushing the narrative of environmental doom to justify these atrocities. Climate change was the perfect excuse to keep people compliant, fearful, and blind.

"They've been prepping for this for decades," he said firmly. "First, they weaken us with food—lacing it with neurotoxins. Then, they control the water, adding chemicals to make us sick. Now, they're targeting the air— saturating it with poisons that change our biology."

He took a deep breath, gaze fixed on the sky, now a patchwork of crisscrossing trails. If they didn't act now, this would be their future—sickness and dependency, a nation of slaves to a tyrannical government.

"They're exterminating us like cockroaches," Jackson said, voice low and dangerous. "And if we don't act soon, there won't be anyone left to fight back."

The gravity of the situation settled over him like a shroud. This wasn't just a battle for freedom—it was a battle for survival. Every man, woman, and child in this country was under attack, their lives slowly snuffed out by the air they breathed.

"There's only one way to protect this country now," he said softly, gaze hardening. "We have to eliminate the true terrorists—the ones hiding in plain sight."

He turned and strode purposefully back toward the safe house, his mind racing with plans. He'd need allies, weapons, and a way to expose the truth to as many people as possible. If they didn't fight back now, they were signing their own death warrants.

"There's a reason our forefathers gave us the right to bear arms," he murmured. "It wasn't just for self-defense— it was to protect us from a tyrannical government."

He glanced back at the sky, where the plane was now a distant speck, its poison spreading slowly across the land.

"America's been sold out," he said grimly. "But if they think we're just going to lie down and die, they've got another thing coming."

Jackson clenched his jaw and headed inside. The time for talking was over. It was time to bring the fight to them.

A List to Save the Nation

Jackson sat in the dimly lit basement of the safehouse, the flickering glow of his laptop screen casting shadows across his face. Outside, the night was still, a deceptive calm that belied the turmoil boiling beneath the surface. He stared at the open document in front of him—a growing list of names, titles, and affiliations.

It was time to face the reality of what needed to be done.

"We tried protests," he muttered to himself. "We tried petitions, debates, everything. And where did that get us?" He clenched his jaw, memories of peaceful rallies turning into violent crackdowns flashing through his mind. "They only tightened the noose."

He took a deep breath, his fingers hovering over the keyboard. This was dangerous territory, and he knew it. The kind of thing that could get him labeled as a domestic terrorist—a target of the very government that was supposed to protect him. But desperate times called for desperate measures. If they didn't fight back now, the whole country would fall.

"There's no turning back," Jackson whispered. "Not anymore."

He tapped a few keys, bringing up the profiles of key figures—faces and names of the people who were orchestrating this nightmare. Politicians, corporate moguls, military brass, media tycoons—each one a crucial cog in the machine that was grinding the nation into submission.

"First up," Jackson said, eyes narrowing as he clicked on a photo of a graying man with a pinched face. "Senator Richard Fallon." Fallon had been one of the loudest voices in favor of the so-called 'Emergency Climate Measures.' He'd spearheaded legislation that granted the government sweeping new powers to control land and resources, all under the guise of environmental protection.

"Fallon's the one shutting down family farms," Jackson muttered, his voice low and dangerous. "Eliminating independent food sources, forcing people to rely on government-approved suppliers. He needs to go."

He added Fallon's name to the list, then moved on to the next face—a woman with sharp eyes and a steely smile.

"Secretary of Health, Amelia Kincaid," he read aloud. "The one behind the medical mandates and health regulations that have crippled half the country." Kincaid's department had been responsible for flooding the market with pharmaceuticals that did more harm than good while suppressing natural remedies and treatments that might have actually helped people. All part of a grand strategy to keep the population dependent and docile.

"Poisoning the people in the name of health," Jackson snarled. "How many have died because of you, Amelia?"

He typed her name into the list, fingers trembling slightly. This was bigger than he'd ever imagined. Every name he added to the document brought them one step closer to dismantling the system—but also one step closer to outright war.

Next, he pulled up a series of documents that detailed the government's use of military assets against its own citizens. He clicked on a blurry photograph of a heavyset man in a military uniform, his face obscured by shadows.

"General Bradley Wexler," Jackson whispered. "Head of the Homeland Security Division. Authorized the use of surveillance drones, armed checkpoints, and direct military force against civilian populations. He's the one keeping the people in check, using fear and force to crush any hint of resistance."

He added Wexler's name to the list, along with every other high-ranking officer and official connected to the military's domestic operations. It was an intricate web of command—a chain of loyalty that would have to be shattered piece by piece if they were ever going to have a chance.

Jackson leaned back, rubbing his eyes. This wasn't just a list of targets. It was a blueprint for freedom, a roadmap to taking back the country from those who had sold it out. He could already see how it would play out—each name on this list represented a different front in the battle. And each one would have to be dealt with swiftly, decisively, before the government could react.

"It's not just about taking them out," Jackson murmured, more to himself than to anyone else. "It's about sending a message. Letting the people know that the fight isn't over, that we still have a chance."

He glanced back at the document, scrolling down the ever-growing list. There were dozens of names now, each one tied to a different aspect of the government's tyranny.

"Chief Justice Ethan Powers," he read, grimacing at the sight of the man's smug smile. Powers had used his position on the Supreme Court to uphold every authoritarian law that crossed his desk, twisting the Constitution to justify each new encroachment on personal freedom.

"He's legalized our enslavement," Jackson said, shaking his head. "Every unconstitutional mandate, every violation of our rights—Powers gave it his stamp of approval. That makes him just as guilty as the rest of them."

The judge's name went on the list, followed by a slew of bureaucrats, lobbyists, and corporate CEOs. Jackson had spent weeks researching each one, pulling on every thread he could find, tracing each piece of legislation, each policy, back to the people responsible. The picture it painted was staggering.

"These aren't just politicians," he muttered. "They're tyrants. Every law they pass, every executive order, every underhanded deal—it's all been building to this. Control the food, control the water, control the air... and you control the people."

But they'd underestimated one thing: the American spirit. The resolve to fight back, even when the odds were stacked against them.

Jackson leaned forward, staring intently at the screen. This was his job now—his responsibility. To protect the people. To honor the oath he'd sworn, not to the government, but to the Constitution and the ideals it represented.

He tapped a few more keys, bringing up the profiles of media moguls—the ones who'd been selling the lies, twisting reality to keep the people asleep. He added their names to the list, each one another stone in the foundation of this corrupt empire.

"We've got the right to bear arms," Jackson whispered, the words a solemn vow. "And it's time we used them. Because if we don't stop these people, no one will."

He paused, his finger hovering over the save button. This document, this list of names, was more than just a plan. It was a death sentence for him and anyone who dared act on it. But he didn't hesitate. He clicked Save, his heart pounding with a fierce, unrelenting resolve.

Jackson knew what had to be done. And he was ready to do whatever it took.

He closed the laptop and stood, his mind already racing with the next steps. Contacts to reach out to, plans to put in place. He'd need a team, people he could trust—people willing to risk everything for the chance to break free.

"One by one, we'll take them down," he said softly, his gaze hard as steel. "And we'll do it in a way they'll never see coming."

With that, he turned and strode out of the basement, the list of names burned into his mind. The war for freedom was about to begin. And Jackson Rivers would lead the charge.

The Burden of Truth

Jackson stood in the cold morning air, the chill biting through his jacket. He could still see the wisps of chemical fog hanging low over the farmlands in the distance, remnants of the planes' early morning run. The fields shimmered with a strange, toxic hue, a grim reminder of just how deep the corruption ran. The government had been poisoning the land for years—slowly, methodically, under the guise of environmental preservation.

The truth was clear: every move they made, every law they passed, was another step toward eradicating freedom and controlling the population. And now that he had the names and faces behind the schemes, Jackson knew what he had to do.

"Time to start spreading the truth," he muttered, setting up his camera on a tripod. He'd found a secure spot, hidden away in a grove of trees, where no drones or surveillance equipment could pick him up. The small, rugged camera in front of him was his only means of communication now—his last line of defense against the relentless propaganda machine.

He took a deep breath, staring into the lens. This was it. The moment he would lay it all bare for the world to see. A message not just to the resistance but to everyone still blind to the lies being fed to them.

"People of America," he began, his voice steady and strong, "I'm Jackson Rivers. You don't know me, but you will. Because today, I'm going to tell you the truth—the truth that's been hidden from you for too long."

He glanced down at the notes he'd scribbled earlier, the pages filled with lines connecting the dots of corruption, greed, and tyranny. "Our government has declared war on us. They've taken our rights, our freedoms, our livelihoods. They're poisoning our food, our water, our air—and they're using your hard-earned money to do it."

Jackson paused, letting the gravity of his words settle. He knew this would be a lot for people to digest. But he had to make them see. He had to make them understand.

"Every paycheck you earn, they take a piece of it. They call it taxes—income tax, property tax, sales tax. They say it's to fund schools, roads, healthcare. But where does it really go? To fund their war machine. To pay for the drones that patrol our skies, for the chemicals that destroy our land, for the surveillance systems that watch our every move."

He leaned closer to the camera, his eyes burning with intensity. "They want you to believe it's for your safety. But it's not. It's for control. Every tax, every regulation, every 'environmental policy'—it's all designed to keep you in line, to keep you compliant, to keep you enslaved."

The wind rustled through the trees, carrying the faint sound of a distant broadcast—a voice droning on about the latest government initiative to combat "climate change." Jackson clenched his fists. It was all connected. The bans on small-scale farming, the endless stream of regulations, the media's unrelenting fear-mongering.

"And it's not just taxes," he continued, voice rising. "They've turned our entire food supply into a weapon.

They've been shutting down farmers, seizing land, and filling our shelves with processed garbage laced with poisons. Look at the labels on your food. Do you even know what half of those chemicals are? You're not supposed to. Because if you did, you'd realize they're not trying to feed you—they're trying to kill you."

Jackson's mind flashed back to that morning's breakfast. The cereal box he'd idly picked up, reading the ingredients list with growing horror. Words he could barely pronounce, chemicals he'd never heard of—all engineered to dumb down the population, to strip away their willpower, to break them.

"It's all part of the plan," he said, voice trembling with barely contained rage. "And it's been going on for years. Decades, even. They've been preparing for this for a long time, making sure that when the time came, we'd be too weak, too distracted, too divided to fight back."

He slammed his fist down on the table, the force rattling the camera. "But not anymore. Not if I have anything to say about it."

Jackson drew a deep breath, regaining his composure. He knew he had to stay calm and focused. This was bigger than him. It was about awakening the people, showing them what was really going on before it was too late.

"They've even started using planes," he said, gesturing to the skies above. "You've seen them—the long trails of mist that hang in the air, the ones they say are 'just condensation.' But they're not. They're spraying chemicals, forever chemicals, over our fields, over our homes. They're seeping into the soil, poisoning our crops, making sure nothing grows without their approval."

He shook his head, the weight of it all crushing down on him. "Global warming? That's the lie they're using to justify it. 'Climate change,' they call it. They want us to believe that it's natural, that it's all just happening on its own. But it's not. It's them. They're using these chemicals to create the illusion of a crisis, to spread fear and keep us begging for their solutions."

Jackson's gaze hardened, his resolve solidifying like steel. "The truth is, they want to eliminate a portion of the population. They want to exterminate us like cockroaches. They've decided that we are the real carbon they need to eliminate, and they'll stop at nothing until we're all gone."

He straightened up, staring directly into the lens. "This is why our forefathers gave us the right to bear arms. Not for hunting, not for sport—but to protect us from a tyrannical government like this one. To defend ourselves when all other options have been exhausted. And I'm telling you now—it might be time to use them."

Jackson let the silence stretch, letting his words hang in the air like a battle cry.

"If you choose to do nothing, you're signing your own death warrant. If you stay silent, you're handing them victory on a silver platter. The time for complacency is over. It's time to stand up. It's time to fight back."

He reached forward, stopping the recording. His heart pounded like a drum, adrenaline surging through his veins. He knew what he was doing was dangerous—treasonous, even in the eyes of those in power. But he didn't care. The people needed to know the truth, and if this was what it took, then so be it.

Jackson hit Upload, sending the video out to every secure channel, every underground network, every resistance group he could find. It would spread like wildfire, reaching eyes and ears that were ready to hear the message.

And once the truth was out, there would be no going back.

Jackson sat hunched over his desk, the harsh light from the monitor casting long shadows on the stacks of papers before him. His heart raced as he sifted through the documents, piecing together the most unsettling truth he had ever encountered. The government's latest health initiative, disguised as a public service, was nothing of the sort. Beneath the surface of the so-called vaccines lay a far more insidious agenda.

On paper, the vaccines appeared to be a benevolent solution to global health threats. But Jackson now knew that each dose wasn't just a safeguard against disease—it was a carefully crafted mechanism for control. The synthetic RNA contained in the injections was not intended only to protect against pathogens. It had been engineered to bind to something far more dangerous: the metals that had been silently building up in the population's bodies for years.

He closed his eyes for a moment, piecing it all together. The government had long ago begun quietly seeding "forever chemicals" into the food, water, and air supply—chemicals laced with trace metals, including iron. These metals didn't just pass through the body; they accumulated, unseen and unnoticed, in human tissues. Over time, the buildup was subtle—imperceptible, even—but now it was everywhere. People had no idea that their bodies had become host to these hidden agents.

The RNA in the vaccines was the key to unlocking the next phase. Jackson's stomach turned as he realized what it meant: this was no longer about protecting the public. It was about controlling them.

Another document clicked open on his screen, and the next phase of the plan was revealed: the rollout of 5G. Publicly, it was a breakthrough in connectivity, promised to revolutionize the world's communication systems. But Jackson saw it for what it truly was: a weapon, silently woven into the fabric of the technological landscape. The electromagnetic waves of 5G, when activated, could interact with the metallic buildup in people's bodies, amplifying those signals. Under certain conditions, the metals embedded in their tissues would begin to react— generating heat, causing pain, and triggering a cascade of debilitating effects.

At first, it would seem like nothing. A slight headache. Nausea. Dizziness. But the potential for escalation was horrifying. With the right conditions, the 5G signals could ignite the metals inside their bodies, turning them into living antennas for the government's control, able to manipulate and inflict harm at will.

To the public, it would all seem like progress. A faster, more efficient world. The promise of a connected society. But to Jackson, it was clear: they were being conditioned to accept a future where they were no longer free. They were becoming conduits for control, their biology turned into the ultimate weapon.

His mind raced as he tried to process what he had uncovered. The government had used every resource, every technological advance, to manipulate the very fabric of human existence. But Jackson wasn't just watching from the sidelines. He was part of the resistance now. And this fight was far from over.

"We can't let them do this," he muttered under his breath, his voice low but filled with determination. "The people don't know what's coming. We have to warn them, but we have to do it quickly."

He knew that exposing the truth wouldn't be easy. The masses had been conditioned for so long, fed lies in the name of progress and health. They had no idea what they had already been subjected to. But Jackson and the resistance were ready to stand against the machine. They couldn't let this new phase of control unfold without a fight.

Jackson looked around the room, his eyes meeting the others' faces. The weight of the situation hung in the air, heavy and unspoken. They had always fought for freedom, but now the stakes had risen. This was no longer just about overthrowing a corrupt government. It was about stopping a technology-driven assault on humanity itself.

"Time's running out," he said, his voice steady but urgent. "We have to move fast. If we can get ahead of this, maybe we can stop it before it's too late."

As Jackson stood, a renewed sense of purpose filled him. The war had shifted in ways he hadn't anticipated, but the resistance was ready. It was no longer just a fight for freedom—it was a battle for survival. They had to expose the truth, awaken the people, and dismantle the system before it took full control. There was no turning back now.

The Education of the Enslaved

Jackson sat back in his chair, the old book resting heavily in his hands, his mind a whirlwind of realization. The truth had always been just out of reach, buried beneath layers of lies and half-truths. He had known for some time that the government was a facade, built to control the masses. But this—this was something deeper, more insidious. The government wasn't just an oppressive force; it was an incubator for ignorance. And the people running it, the ones who enforced the rules and kept the gears turning, were the most dangerous of them all. They weren't evil masterminds. No, they were something far worse: educated idiots.

Jackson had spent years studying the system, unraveling the lies they fed him from birth. But nothing prepared him for the depths of their deception. The more he observed the bureaucrats and public servants, the more he saw a terrifying pattern. The ones with the most degrees, the highest positions, the most so-called knowledge—they were the worst. Their education had done nothing but blind them, deaden their senses to the truth, and make them complicit in the very system they should have been questioning.

The deeper their schooling, the more they had lost their ability to think for themselves. It was as though they were taught to shut off their critical thinking, to trust the system no matter what. The higher the education, the lower the capacity for free thought. And it wasn't by accident. It was deliberate. They had been conditioned to believe that the world worked in a way that only made sense to the few who could manipulate the system. They couldn't see it, though.

They had been trained to accept things at face value, to trust authority without question, and to mindlessly follow instructions like obedient machines. And when you tried to show them the truth, their first reaction was denial, as if their minds couldn't even process the possibility that the entire system they had devoted their lives to was a lie.

Jackson could see it in their eyes. The government employees—the ones pushing paper and making decisions about people's lives—were no better than zombies. Their minds, once vibrant with curiosity, had been drained by years of indoctrination, and now they had become little more than shells of the people they once could have been. They went through school like obedient cattle, fed the same tired, empty propaganda over and over again. They were rewarded for memorizing facts and spitting them back out, never once questioning the underlying assumptions that shaped their world. These people were educated, sure, but educated in the wrong things. Their knowledge wasn't real; it was just a set of instructions to keep them compliant.

The truth about money—the fact that gold and silver were the only real forms of currency, as dictated by the Constitution—had been hidden from them. They had been taught to use paper, to accept Federal Reserve notes as if they held some value, when in reality they were no more valuable than the ink that printed them. And this wasn't just ignorance—it was willful blindness. They were paid in paper, a worthless commodity, and they worked for it like slaves without even realizing it. They didn't understand that this paper was the chain that kept them in their place, in their little box, doing the bidding of the powers that be.

What was worse, they had been drugged and manipulated into believing this was the only way. Doctors, complicit in the scheme, pushed their shots and pills, not to cure or heal, but to dull their senses and dull their minds. The vaccinations, the chemicals in their food, the fluoride in their water—every dose was another step toward cognitive submission. It was like they were trained to forget how to think, to lose the ability to question, to numb themselves into accepting a world where paper was real money, where lies were truth, and where freedom was just a word with no meaning. And the more shots they took, the less they cared. It wasn't just a physical ailment; it was a spiritual and mental paralysis.

They weren't the ones controlling the system; they were the ones being used by it. The ones who worked for the state had become the pawns, the cannon fodder in a game they didn't even understand. The more they tried to climb the ladder, the more they became part of the problem. They weren't the elite pulling the strings. They weren't the ones who had the power to shape the world. No, they were the ones being controlled, just like everyone else. They just didn't know it. They believed they had power because they had paper to wave in people's faces. But the truth was, they were as much slaves to the system as the ones they oppressed.

Jackson could see it in their actions, the way they mindlessly filed paperwork, the way they pushed through policies that harmed people without ever questioning them. They had been taught that their job was to enforce the rules, no matter how unjust or ridiculous. And yet, they didn't know that by doing so, they were participating in the very corruption that had stripped them of their dignity. They had become the worst of them all—educated, but not intelligent.

Knowledgeable, but not wise. They had been taught to follow, never to lead.

But Jackson understood now. He understood that the more they were "educated," the less they actually knew. They were no longer capable of understanding the world as it was—they were too indoctrinated, too blinded by their own need to fit in, to question the truth. And that, in the end, was what made them so dangerous.

As he pieced together the grand conspiracy, it became clearer than ever: it wasn't just the corrupt elites who were to blame. It was the system itself, one that had hollowed out the minds of the very people meant to uphold the law. Jackson knew now that the only way to break free was to awaken the ones who had been lulled into a false sense of security by their degrees and titles. To show them that they were not the enlightened ones, but the most deeply deceived. And once they saw the truth, once they understood that they had been living a lie, they would be the ones to tear the whole system down.

Jackson's resolve solidified. The battle was no longer just about him. It was about waking up the millions of souls who had been lulled into complacency, who had been made to believe that their paper was real, that their education had freed them, when in reality it had bound them in chains.

The revolution, Jackson realized, wouldn't just be fought in the streets. It would be fought in the minds of those who had been blinded by the very system they were protecting. They had to know the truth. And he was going to make sure they did.

Taking Aim

The low hum of Jackson's laptop filled the room as he watched his video go live across dozens of encrypted platforms. He could already see comments flooding in, messages of support mixed with confusion and disbelief. People were waking up, but they were still too scared, too overwhelmed to act.

That's why he needed more than words—he needed a plan.

Jackson moved to a cluttered desk in the corner of his safehouse, rifling through papers, maps, and notes. Each piece of information represented a step in the government's control scheme. But he wasn't interested in theory anymore. He needed something tangible—names, locations, weaknesses. He had to show the people that there was a way to fight back.

He flipped through a manila folder marked with the word Priority. It contained a list he'd put together over the last few weeks, gathering information from whistleblowers, resistance contacts, and even disgruntled former officials. The names on this list were the architects of the government's plan—bureaucrats, CEOs, and military generals, all pulling the strings behind the scenes.

"Here's where it starts," he whispered to himself. "Cut off the head, and the body falls."

Jackson's eyes scanned the names, each one like a puzzle piece clicking into place.

1. Senator Richard Hawthorne: The public face of the government's "Climate Change Initiative." He was the one pushing for the shutdown of family farms and promoting the use of genetically modified crops laced with poisons.
2. General Matthew Grayson: Head of the military's domestic operations. He commanded the fleet of planes dispersing chemicals over farmland and suburban neighborhoods.
3. Elizabeth Kane: CEO of Global Harvest, the conglomerate that had systematically bought out independent farms, enforcing strict guidelines that made it impossible to grow natural, healthy crops.
4. Director William Sloane: Leader of the National Surveillance Agency, in charge of the country's surveillance grid. Every move Jackson made, every call, every message—it all passed through Sloane's network.
5. Chief Justice Robert Whitaker: The one who ensured that every lawsuit, every challenge against the government's unconstitutional actions, was dismissed before it could even reach the public's eyes.

Jackson scribbled down more details, mapping out each target's role in the overall plan. It wasn't enough to expose them—he had to dismantle the system they'd built, brick by brick. And that meant taking these people out of the equation permanently.

"First things first," he murmured, tapping his pen against the page. "Elizabeth Kane."

She was the easiest to reach, the least protected. Her office in the city was a fortress. Still, she frequently attended "public outreach" events, using them as a platform to spread propaganda about the necessity of chemical-laden food production. Jackson had seen footage of her at these events—smiling, shaking hands, spreading her lies.

If he could get close to her and make a statement, it would send a message to the others. It would show them that no one was untouchable and that the people were ready to fight back.

He dialed a number on his secure line, waiting for the familiar voice on the other end.

"Yeah?" the voice grunted.

"It's Rivers. I need a location for Elizabeth Kane's next appearance. And I need it fast."

There was a pause, then the sound of typing. "Hold on. I've got something. She's scheduled to give a speech at the North District Agriculture Fair tomorrow. Security's tight but not impenetrable."

"Perfect," Jackson said, his mind already working through the logistics. "Get me blueprints of the venue, guard schedules, and any other intel you have. I'll take it from there."

"You got it, man. But… be careful, alright? These people don't play around."

Jackson hung up without responding. He knew the risks. He'd seen what happened to those who stood up and failed—disappearances, suicides that weren't suicides, accidents that were anything but accidental.

But this wasn't about him anymore. This was about every farmer forced off their land, every family bankrupted by taxes, and every citizen breathing in toxic air and drinking poisoned water. If someone had to put their life on the line to bring these people down, it might as well be him.

He spent the next few hours preparing—assembling his gear, checking his weapons, going over the plan again and again. He'd need to be quick and precise. One shot was all he'd get, and it had to count.

As the sun dipped below the horizon, Jackson locked and loaded his pistol, securing it in a shoulder holster. He slipped a small blade into his boot and a vial of sedative into his jacket pocket. He didn't know what would happen tomorrow, but he was ready for anything.

Before he left, he glanced at the list one more time. After Kane, there would be others. General Grayson. Director Sloane. Senator Hawthorne. One by one, they'd all fall.

"Time to fight back," he whispered, turning away from the list and stepping into the darkness outside. He had a job to do—a war to wage.

And he was just getting started.

Unveiling the Puppeteer

The small room was dark, the only light coming from a single lamp illuminating Jackson's desk. He sifted through the new stack of documents, each page detailing more layers of the conspiracy. Every piece of information felt like a fresh wound, deepening his resolve to expose the corruption rotting the core of the nation.

A knock at the door pulled his attention away. Jackson tensed, his hand moving instinctively to the pistol resting on the table. He never got visitors at the safehouse unless it was urgent.

"Who is it?" he called out cautiously.

"It's Marcus. Got something you need to see." The voice on the other side was low and familiar, a fellow resistance member and trusted ally.

Jackson eased up and unlocked the door, letting Marcus in. The older man entered quickly, closing the door behind him. He looked exhausted, his face lined with stress and dark circles under his eyes.

"What's going on?" Jackson asked.

Marcus held up a flash drive, his expression grim. "Intel from one of our inside sources. A new player joined the game. Someone with a lot of power and a hell of a lot of money."

Jackson's brow furrowed as he plugged the drive into his laptop. He opened the folder labeled URGENT and scanned through the files. Diagrams of genetically engineered crops, memos from high-level meetings, investment portfolios—

each piece painting a clearer picture of what they were up against.

"Who is he?" Jackson asked, leaning closer to the screen. "Name's, Gates. William, Gates,"Marcus replied.

"Billionaire philanthropist turned...well, something else entirely. Started buying up farmland a few years ago, then launched a company called Appeal. Their mission is supposedly to 'enhance food sustainability' or some crap like that. But the reality is much darker."

Jackson clicked on a video file. The grainy footage showed Gates at a conference, standing behind a podium emblazoned with the Appeal logo. He was speaking to an audience of bureaucrats and corporate leaders, his tone calm and composed as he explained his vision.

"We must face the facts," Gates said, his voice smooth and practiced. "Traditional farming methods are simply unsustainable for the future. We need to think beyond organic agriculture, beyond conventional practices. With Appeal, we're introducing cutting-edge technologies that will revolutionize how we produce food—cleaner, safer, and more nutritious."

Jackson paused the video, staring at Gates's serene smile frozen on the screen. Something was chilling about it—an emptiness in his eyes as if he believed every lie he was telling.

"What's his angle?" Jackson asked, glancing at Marcus. "Control," Marcus answered flatly. "He's already

bought out a significant portion of America's remaining independent farms. And it's not just about owning the land—it's about what he's doing to it."

He handed Jackson another file, this one filled with lab reports and chemical analyses. Jackson flipped through it, his eyes widening with each page.

"Holy…these compounds…" Jackson trailed off, shaking his head in disbelief. "This isn't food enhancement. It's a slow-acting poison."

"Exactly," Marcus said, his voice low. "Appeal is introducing a new form of synthetic coating on fruits and vegetables. They call it an 'edible protective layer,' but it's designed to do more than just preserve freshness. It alters the chemical composition of the food, making it addictive, but also introducing toxins that build up over time. Weakens the immune system, disrupts hormones… you name it."

"And no one's questioning it?" Jackson asked, his anger simmering beneath the surface. "No one's investigating what they're putting into our food?"

"Who's going to question the man funding the entire agricultural reform?" Marcus replied bitterly. "He's got the

FDA in his pocket. Politicians on both sides of the aisle sing his praises. He's funding research, scholarships—hell, he's even got his own foundation providing 'nutritional aid' to third-world countries."

Jackson stood up, pacing the small room. The scope of it all was staggering. Gates wasn't just another wealthy elite pulling strings from behind the scenes. He was engineering the very fabric of society, altering the food supply to keep people subdued, all under the pretense of humanitarian aid.

"And the resistance?" Jackson asked. "Are they aware of this?"

"Not fully," Marcus admitted. "But they will be. Once they know who's behind the poison in their food, it'll light a fire under them. People are fed up with the government, but this guy? He's even worse. He's not elected. He's not accountable. He's a shadow figure, controlling the narrative through billions of dollars and a smiling face on TV."

Jackson stared at the image of Gates on the screen. He'd taken out corrupt politicians before, exposed government lies, but this—this was something new. Gates was an outsider with a reach that extended far beyond Washington. His influence seeped into every home, every grocery store, every meal.

"So, what's the plan?" Jackson asked, his voice hardening.

"We expose him. We hit him where it hurts—his public image. People see him as a hero, a philanthropist. We show them the truth, and we break that illusion."

"And if that doesn't work?"

Marcus's eyes met Jackson's, and the unspoken words hung between them.

Then we take him out.

"First, we need to gather more evidence," Marcus said. "Detailed reports, testimonies—proof that no one can deny. Then we leak it and spread it across every channel we have. Gates is big, but he's not invincible. If we can turn the people against him, we can shut Appeal down for good."

Jackson nodded slowly, his mind racing with possibilities. Taking down Gates would be no small feat, but it was a necessary one. If they didn't stop him now, there'd be nothing left to save.

"Alright," Jackson said, determination solidifying his voice. "Let's get to work. And when the time comes...we make sure Gates knows he's not untouchable."

Marcus nodded, a grim smile crossing his face. "It's about time someone reminded him."

Jackson unplugged the flash drive and tucked it into his pocket. The battle against the government's tyranny was far from over, but a new front had opened up. Gates thought he was untouchable, a master puppeteer pulling strings in the shadows.

But Jackson would show him what happened when those strings snapped.

As the two men left the safehouse, Jackson felt a new sense of purpose building inside him. This wasn't just about saving lives anymore—it was about taking the fight to those who thought they could control the world.

And no one, not even a billionaire like Gates, would be safe from the storm that was coming.

Lines in the Sand

Jackson sat at the edge of a weather-beaten wooden bench; his gaze fixed on the crowded city square before him. The North District buzzed with activity—families strolling through the open-air markets, kids chasing each other around a fountain, and vendors hawking everything from fresh produce to handmade crafts. It looked normal enough, a snapshot of small-town America, but Jackson knew appearances were deceiving.

The North District Agriculture Fair was set to host Elizabeth Kane's speech today. But more importantly, it was an opportunity for Jackson to observe the layout and security before making his next move. He knew taking down Kane would only be the beginning. Exposing Gates and Appeal was a much larger challenge, but Jackson needed to start somewhere.

He glanced at the large screen set up on a stage in the distance. A slideshow flickered to life, highlighting the supposed "advancements" Appeal had made in food production. The audience cheered as images of gleaming, engineered produce appeared on the screen.

Jackson gritted his teeth. The same people applauding Kane's efforts had no idea that each bite of fruit they consumed came laced with microscopic toxins—just enough to disrupt their health slowly, over months and years, until they were too sick, too docile to resist.

"That's it, folks!" a loudspeaker boomed, catching Jackson's attention. "Join us in an hour for an exclusive keynote speech by Elizabeth Kane herself. Learn how

Appeal is transforming our food industry and ensuring a sustainable future for generations to come!"

The crowd erupted into cheers again. Jackson's jaw tightened. He had an urge to stand up, to shout the truth, but he knew it would only get him arrested or worse. This wasn't the time for rash actions. He needed to play it smart.

As he stood to leave, his burner phone buzzed in his pocket. He pulled it out and glanced at the message:

Need to talk. Meet me at 5th and Main. Urgent.

It was Marcus. Jackson slipped away from the square and made his way to the rendezvous point, navigating through narrow alleys and side streets until he spotted Marcus leaning against a lamppost.

"What's up?" Jackson asked, glancing around to make sure they weren't being watched.

"We've got a problem," Marcus muttered, shoving a folder into Jackson's hands. "It's about Gates. He's not just targeting food production. It's bigger than that."

Jackson flipped through the folder, his eyes widening as he skimmed the contents. It contained a series of schematics, blueprints for distribution centers scattered across the country, each one marked with symbols and acronyms Jackson had never seen before.

"What the hell is all this?" he asked, looking up at Marcus.

"Poison hubs," Marcus explained grimly. "Gates has been setting up these facilities all over the nation. They're disguised as food processing centers, but in reality, they're outfitted with equipment for mass chemical distribution."

Jackson's stomach twisted. "Mass chemical distribution? You mean… they're planning to contaminate the entire food supply?"

"Not just the food," Marcus said, lowering his voice. "Water, too. They've been running tests in select cities, adding compounds that disrupt cognitive function and make people more susceptible to suggestion. It's why people aren't questioning the rise in illnesses, why they're so willing to accept every new policy without a fight."

Jackson clenched his fists. He'd known the situation was bad, but this—it was worse than he'd imagined. If Gates succeeded, there'd be no one left to resist. The chemicals would weaken them and break them down until they were nothing more than obedient drones.

"Alright," Jackson said slowly, a dark determination settling over him. "Where do we start?"

Marcus pointed to a map inside the folder, highlighting a location near the coast. "There's a facility outside of Charleston. Small, heavily guarded, but it's where they're conducting their initial water tests. If we can get inside, gather evidence, and shut it down, it'll send a message to Gates and his cronies."

Jackson nodded. "Then we do it. We'll need a team, equipment, and an exit strategy."

"I've already got a few people on standby," Marcus said. "We'll meet tonight at the old dockyard. But Jackson… there's one more thing you need to know."

"What?"

Marcus hesitated, then handed Jackson a grainy photograph. It showed Gates shaking hands with a man

Jackson didn't recognize—a tall, broad-shouldered figure with a military bearing.

"Who's this?" Jackson asked.

"General Bradford," Marcus replied. "Runs a private security firm called Iron Shield. They've been providing muscle for Gates's operations. He's got ex-special forces, mercenaries… guys who won't hesitate to kill if you get in their way."

Jackson studied the photograph, memorizing the general's face. Iron Shield. So Gates wasn't just relying on corporate influence and government corruption—he had a private army backing him up.

"This changes things," Jackson muttered. "We'll need to be careful. But if we can take down one of these poison hubs, it'll be a major blow."

Marcus nodded. "We'll be ready. Just… watch your back, Jackson. These people aren't playing games."

"I know," Jackson said quietly. He folded the map and tucked it into his jacket, his mind racing with strategies and scenarios.

As Marcus turned to leave, Jackson glanced back at the city square. Elizabeth Kane would be giving her speech soon, spreading more lies and drawing more people into Gates's web. But after tonight, things would be different.

The resistance had taken their first real step. And Jackson would make sure that Gates knew they weren't going to back down.

"Tonight," he whispered to himself. "We make our stand."

With that, Jackson disappeared into the shadows, his resolve hardened. The battle for America's soul had begun, and he wasn't going to let Gates and his accomplices poison the people's future without a fight.

The Rising Tide

News of the Charleston operation spread like wildfire. Jackson hadn't anticipated it happening so quickly. As the footage and data his team leaked hit underground networks and back channels, something incredible began to happen. The evidence of Gates's poison hub went viral— uncovering the dark truth behind the Appeal, the government, and the manipulation of the food and water supply.

It wasn't just the resistance movement paying attention now.

People everywhere—ordinary citizens, veterans, farmers, even former law enforcement—watched in shock as Jackson's footage revealed tanks of chemicals hidden in the food processing plant. Test results showed how the compounds interfered with the nervous system, cognitive abilities, and even reproductive health. For many, this was the breaking point. They'd had enough of the lies, the manipulations, and the covert poisoning of their countrymen.

Across the country, pockets of resistance began to form.

At first, it was small-scale—graffiti on billboards denouncing Gates and his conspirators, sabotage of distribution centers tied to chemical dispersal, and protests outside city halls and government buildings. But as the days passed, the unrest escalated.

In a dimly lit garage in Houston, a group of construction workers and mechanics watched the footage on an old television set. Their faces were a mix of rage and determination.

"They think they can just poison us and get away with it?" one man spat, slamming a fist into his palm.

"No more," another said. "If the government doesn't protect us, then we protect ourselves."

Elsewhere, in the farmlands of the Midwest, farmers banded together. They had been pushed to the brink—land seized under the guise of "environmental protection," water sources poisoned, and crops ruined. When the news of Gates's poison hubs reached them, it was like a match igniting dry tinder.

"They want to control the food supply?" one farmer, a grizzled man named Earl, told a gathering crowd on his property. "Then they'll have to pry it from our cold, dead hands. We're not going down without a fight."

Men and women nodded in agreement. Their tractors and combines weren't just tools for farming anymore—they became barriers and makeshift armored vehicles to protect what little they had left. They formed roadblocks on highways leading to suspected chemical facilities, defying local authorities to stop them.

Word spread quickly through online forums, encrypted chat groups, and whispered conversations in quiet corners of bars and coffee shops. People who had never considered themselves fighters, who had never even owned a gun, were now arming themselves. They weren't going to let their families be slowly poisoned. They weren't going to sit by while their neighbors were weakened and broken down.

In Arizona, a group of bikers known for their community work repurposed their organization into a mobile unit targeting government operations. They rode through the state's backroads, hitting checkpoints and small offices suspected of collaborating with Gates's operations. They weren't looking for a fight, but they were ready if one came to them.

On the East Coast, an underground journalist known only as "The Voice" became a beacon for those seeking action. Broadcasting from a hidden location, his distorted voice crackled through radios and online streams, galvanizing listeners with messages of defiance and hope.

"America was built on the backs of those who refused to be slaves," he said in one broadcast. "Our forefathers fought, bled, and died to ensure we'd never bow to tyranny. Well, look around. The tyrants are back, poisoning our land, our food, our minds. They think we're too weak, too stupid to see it. But we see it now. And we're done being their puppets. It's time to cut the strings."

His broadcasts, combined with the evidence Jackson had leaked, created a ripple effect. People who had once felt isolated, scared, and hopeless began to realize they weren't alone. They weren't crazy for thinking something was wrong. There were others out there just like them, ready to stand up and fight back.

The turning point came two weeks after the Charleston raid.

Jackson and Marcus were holed up in a safe house, watching the latest broadcast. They had been lying low, waiting for the dust to settle. But as they watched footage of protestors storming a government office in Nevada and burning the symbol of the Appeal in effigy, Marcus turned to Jackson with a look of disbelief.

"You see this?" Marcus muttered; eyes wide. "This is more than just a few protests. It's everywhere. People are… really fighting back."

Jackson nodded slowly, a flicker of satisfaction crossing his face. "They needed a spark, that's all. Just something to wake them up. But this is just the beginning."

The footage shifted to a shaky cellphone video showing a group of armed citizens surrounding a convoy of black SUVs. Shouts erupted, and the men inside the vehicles were pulled out, one by one. The cameraman zoomed in on a face Jackson recognized instantly—one of Gates's top lieutenants, a man overseeing operations in three states.

"This is for our families!" a voice shouted off-screen, followed by the ominous sound of gunfire. The video cut out abruptly, leaving only stunned silence.

Marcus turned to Jackson, his expression grave. "People are starting to take matters into their own hands. What if it gets out of control?"

Jackson leaned back, rubbing his chin thoughtfully. "It was never going to be clean, Marcus. Once people start waking up, there's no telling what they'll do. But that's the risk we had to take. Gates needs to see that the people aren't his pawns—they're the storm that's going to tear him down."

Marcus nodded, processing Jackson's words. "So, what's the next step?"

"We escalate," Jackson said, his voice steely. "We need to hit another hub—one of their major distribution centers. We can't just sit back and watch. We need to lead by example. Show them that even the most fortified targets can fall."

He glanced at a map spread across the table, his eyes locking onto a heavily marked location.

"Philadelphia," he murmured. "There's a distribution hub there. Massive. Supplies a quarter of the East Coast. If we can take it down…"

"We cripple their entire network," Marcus finished, his voice filled with a mix of excitement and fear.

Jackson nodded, the fire of resolve burning in his eyes. "Exactly. And this time, we're not just going in to gather evidence. We're going to send a message."

The resistance had been born in the shadows, but now it was coming into the light. The people were rising, and Jackson was ready to lead them into the heart of the storm. It was time to show Gates and his cronies what happened when America's people decided they'd had enough.

Taking Down the Giants

The night air was thick with tension as Jackson sat silently in the back of a nondescript delivery truck, his mind running through the plan for the hundredth time. The vehicle rattled softly as it made its way through the dark, narrow streets of Philadelphia, the city's industrial district looming ahead.

"Ten minutes to drop point," Rourke's voice crackled over the comms, breaking the silence.

Jackson glanced around the dimly lit interior. Packed tight were nearly two dozen men and women, all armed to the teeth and clad in dark tactical gear. Some were veterans, hardened by years of service; others were ordinary citizens fed up with watching their country be bled dry by the powerful and corrupt. Tonight, they were united by a single purpose—taking down one of Gates's largest distribution hubs.

"This is it," Jackson muttered, his voice low but firm. "This is where we hit them where it hurts. They think they're untouchable, hiding behind layers of security and secrecy. Tonight, we show them how wrong they are."

The faces around him were set in grim determination. No one spoke. There was nothing left to say.

The truck came to a stop, and Rourke slid open the back door, peering out cautiously. The street was deserted, the only sound the distant hum of machinery from the nearby warehouses. Jackson climbed out first, scanning the area.

They were just a block away from the target—a massive, heavily guarded facility, hidden in plain sight among the other industrial buildings.

"Everyone knows the plan," Jackson whispered as the rest of the team filed out. "We split into two squads. Marcus, you take Alpha Team around back. Cut the power and take out the external cameras. Rourke and I will go with Bravo Team through the front. We'll create enough chaos to draw their attention, giving Alpha Team the opening they need to get to the control room."

"Copy that," Marcus said, his eyes glinting with adrenaline. "Just make sure you leave a few for us."

Jackson managed a faint smile. "No promises."

They moved quickly, splitting into their respective teams. The shadows swallowed them as they made their way toward the facility's perimeter. Jackson's heart pounded in his chest, but his mind was calm and clear. He'd been in worse situations before, but never had so much been on the line.

They reached the chain-link fence that surrounded the facility. Rourke took point, expertly snipping through the metal links with a pair of bolt cutters. The team slipped through the opening one by one, creeping silently across the yard toward the towering structure ahead.

Jackson raised his hand, signaling a halt as they neared the main gate. Two armed guards stood watch, scanning the area with bored expressions.

"Two targets, front entrance," Jackson whispered into his mic. "Take 'em down quietly."

Rourke nodded, shouldering his rifle and taking aim. With a soft thwap, the first guard crumpled to the ground, a tranquilizer dart embedded in his neck. The second barely had time to react before he, too, was down, his body slumping against the gate.

"Clear," Rourke murmured, motioning for the team to move forward.

They slipped through the front gate, moving swiftly and silently across the yard. As they approached the main entrance, Jackson glanced over his shoulder at the distant outline of Marcus and Alpha Team positioning themselves at the rear of the building.

"All teams in position," Jackson said quietly. "Alpha, get ready to cut the power on my mark."

"Copy that," Marcus's voice crackled back.

Jackson took a deep breath, steadying himself. "Three… two… one… mark."

A second later, the entire facility was plunged into darkness. The lights flickered out, and a chorus of startled shouts echoed from inside. Jackson wasted no time, motioning for Bravo Team to breach the front door.

The door burst open with a loud crash, and they were in.

Gunfire erupted as guards scrambled to react, but Jackson and his team were already moving, taking down targets with ruthless efficiency. Bullets ricocheted off steel and concrete as they pushed forward, sweeping through the entrance hall and into the main warehouse.

The place was a maze of towering shelves and industrial machinery, and in the darkness, it was easy to get disoriented. But Jackson had memorized the layout. He led the team through the labyrinthine corridors, cutting down guards and security personnel as they went.

"Alpha Team, status?" Jackson barked into his mic. "Almost at the control room," Marcus replied, the sound of gunfire and shouting in the background. "We've got heavy resistance here. They must've had backup on standby."

"Hold them off. We're heading your way."

Jackson signaled to his team, and they altered course, cutting through a side corridor to flank the guards converging on Alpha Team. As they rounded a corner, they came face-to-face with a squad of heavily armed men. The air filled with the deafening roar of gunfire as both sides opened up.

Jackson dropped to one knee, squeezing off shots with deadly precision. Rourke was a whirlwind of motion beside him, his rifle barking as he laid down suppressive fire. The guards didn't stand a chance. Within moments, the corridor was littered with bodies, and the way to the control room was clear.

"Move up!" Jackson shouted.

They pushed forward, reaching the control room just as Marcus and Alpha Team broke through the opposite door. The guards inside scrambled to defend, but the combined force of both teams overwhelmed them.

"Secure the door!" Jackson ordered as the last guard went down. He turned to Marcus, who was already at the control console, typing furiously.

"Got it," Marcus said triumphantly, pulling up a screen filled with data. "This is it. Inventory logs, distribution routes, and chemical analysis reports. It's all here."

"Download everything," Jackson said, glancing around. "We don't have much time."

Marcus plugged in a portable drive and began the transfer. As they waited, Jackson's mind raced. This data could blow the lid off Gates's entire operation. It was proof of the poisoning, of the deliberate contamination of food and water supplies across the country. Once they got it out, there would be no denying what was happening.

But even as the drive filled with incriminating files, Jackson knew this was only the beginning. Exposing the truth was one thing—taking down the people behind it was another.

The download finished, and Marcus yanked the drive free. "We're good to go."

"Alright," Jackson said, his voice firm. "Let's get out of here."

Just as they turned to leave, a new voice crackled over the facility's intercom system.

"Going somewhere?"

Jackson froze, eyes narrowing as he recognized the smooth, almost amused tone.

"Gates," he muttered.

The intercom crackled again. "You really think I didn't see this coming? You're not the only ones who can plan ahead, you know. But go ahead—take your little prize. It won't matter in the end. This is just one hub, and you're just a handful of rebels. The wheels are already in motion, Jackson. You can't stop it."

Jackson clenched his fists, fury boiling in his chest. "We'll see about that."

The intercom went silent. Jackson exchanged a look with Marcus and the others. There was no time to waste. They needed to get out before reinforcements arrived.

"Let's move!" Jackson barked.

They fought their way back out, gunfire and shouts echoing through the night. As they broke free of the facility and melted into the darkness, Jackson knew one thing for certain:

The fight was far from over. But the people were waking up, and soon, Gates would realize just how much power they really had.

Tonight, had been a victory. But tomorrow would be the real test.

www.ingramcontent.com/pod-product-compliance
Lightning Source LLC
LaVergne TN
LVHW051954060526
838201LV00059B/3632
* 9 7 9 8 3 4 8 5 6 4 7 5 9 *